"This handbook for happiness is as clear and accurate as ^ ·
wish but written in a language—and with ? ·
Simpson would enjoy. A rare achieve

"This is a wonderful book about the pursu   ...cn precisely for
the average Joe. It presents the perennial v..souom of Aristotle's *Nicomachean
Ethics* in a manner that is fun to read and easy to understand by non-philos-
ophers. . . . Written with a somewhat ironic and jesting tone and down-to-
earth examples, it will be especially attractive to a younger audience."

—JOHN GOYETTE
Thomas Aquinas College

"*Advice from Aristotle* provides a refreshingly accessible, acerbic, and
thoughtful introduction to Aristotle's system of moral philosophy. . . .
Rigorous but fun, this book is a must-read for anyone interested in living a
more fulfilling life."

—KRISTOPHER G. PHILLIPS
Southern Utah University

"Since Aristotle emphasizes the importance of 'finding a balance,' it's fitting that *Advice from Aristotle* strikes the perfect balance of clarity, humor,
and accessibility on the one hand and careful representation of the original
Aristotelian spirit on the other. Whether it's someone's first time encoun-
tering Aristotle or their hundredth, *Advice from Aristotle* is sure to inspire
readers to appreciate the broad applicability of Aristotle's ideas to twenty-
first-century life."

—CASSIE L. FINLEY
PhD candidate, University of Iowa

Advice from Aristotle

Advice from Aristotle

Life Lessons from the *Nicomachean Ethics*

Andrew Younan

CASCADE *Books* · Eugene, Oregon

ADVICE FROM ARISTOTLE
Life Lessons from the *Nicomachean Ethics*

Cascade Books
An Imprint of Wipf and Stock Publishers
199 W. 8th Ave., Suite 3
Eugene, OR 97401

www.wipfandstock.com

PAPERBACK ISBN: 978-1-6667-3540-6
HARDCOVER ISBN: 978-1-6667-9244-7
EBOOK ISBN: 978-1-6667-9245-4

Cataloguing-in-Publication data:

Names: Younan, Andrew [author].

Title: Advice from Aristotle : life lessons from the *Nicomachean Ethics* / Andrew Younan.

Description: Eugene, OR: Cascade Books, 2022 | Includes bibliographical references and index.

Identifiers: ISBN 978-1-6667-3540-6 (paperback) | ISBN 978-1-6667-9244-7 (hardcover) | ISBN 978-1-6667-9245-4 (ebook)

Subjects: LCSH: Aristotle. Nicomachean ethics | Ethics, Ancient | Aristotle | Ethics | Happiness | Conduct of life

Classification: B430 Y68 2022 (print) | B430 (ebook)

04/20/22

Illustrations by Ruvianne Mercado

To my garbage people.

Contents

Introduction

If you never want to feel sad again, this is the book for you.

That's what I'd say if I were more interested in selling a book than telling the truth. But I don't have a bridge to sell you, or an amazing diet pill, or guaranteed happiness. The truth is just the opposite: I can basically guarantee that you'll be sad again, because that's life, and anyone telling you otherwise really is just trying to sell you something. Some sad things are entirely out of your control, like death and all of human history and skinny jeans. Some are partially in your control, like pollution and hangovers and your friends being mad at you for what you did on Friday. I'll have a lot to say about a lot of this, but I don't want to mislead you into thinking there's some trick to never feeling sad again. This book isn't ultimately about feeling happy or sad (or at least, it's not only about that). It's about becoming a certain kind of person: the kind of person who can know and choose and feel what's best in the infinitely varying situations of everyday life. Feeling good for a while, or knowing something, or doing a good thing, are all pretty easy and short-lived things. Becoming a certain kind of person (I'll be using the word "virtuous" pretty soon) is hard and takes time. But there's nothing more worth it, and living virtuously is about as close as anyone can get to actual happiness in a world that can be pretty lousy. And as a bonus, if you want to make the world a less-lousy place, you'll need lots of virtue for that too.

The Great Book that this hopefully half-decent book is based on was probably written around 330 B.C. by Aristotle, student of Plato, student of Socrates. It's called the *Nicomachean Ethics* (I'll sometimes imprecisely call it the *Ethics*), dedicated by Aristotle to his son Nicomachus, whom I don't know anything about. It's not important as far as this book is concerned, since whoever Nicomachus was, he was a human being, and this book, like the book it's based on, is about human beings and what it means for them to live happy lives.

Anyone who knows me could tell you that I am no expert on good living, or virtue, or happiness. I try, I suppose, but not always even that. In any case, that's not important either, since this book is not about my wisdom, but Aristotle's. It seems to me that he had quite a bit of it. If you find any wisdom in this book, it's his, not mine, and you should read what he has to say for himself. If you don't like this book, that's my fault, not his, and you should read what he has to say for himself. Either way, read Aristotle. Or don't. It will make no difference to me, and it'll just be your loss.

Nerd notes: first, this is not a commentary. Commentaries are generally boring and written for a scholarly audience, and engage scholarly debates about the text. I actively avoid such debates, both in real life and in this book, and at most will give suggestions or hints at what I think some answers might be to the exegetical issues of Aristotle's text. This is a practical book for non-experts, though I hope it's interesting to everyone, including philosophy nerds (real ones, not just people on Twitter). I think writing a practical book about the *Nicomachean Ethics* is just what Aristotle would have wanted

Figure 1: The man

for his book, because he says himself that ethics is about action, not just sitting around thinking. I have some thoughts on popular writing in general in the Appendix for anyone interested. Finally, when I quote the text I'll be using the translation of W. D. Ross, both because it's pretty good for my purposes and because it's copyright free.

Ok, let's see if an ancient Greek can still teach us something about being human.

— Book I —

Happiness

In This Chapter:

Selfishness, imprecision, fake happiness, real happiness, emotions.

Not All About You

> "For even if the end is the same for a single man and for a state, that of the state seems at all events something greater and more complete whether to attain or to preserve; though it is worthwhile to attain the end merely for one man, it is finer and more godlike to attain it for a nation or for city-states." (I.2)

Let's get something out of the way from the start. Be happy and do what it takes to get happy, but you're not the center of the world, and because other people are just as important as you are, the good of everyone is way more important than the good of just you. So if it comes down to your happiness and the happiness of the world or country or community you live in, get ready to be disappointed, and make your best effort to grow up and get over yourself.

I prefer to use stupid examples. I'm often late when I drive somewhere, and my lateness causes me to be grumpy, and my grumpiness apparently causes every street light to turn red when I get near it. This creates a cycle of anger at the city planner who apparently timed the red lights on purpose just to spite me, then hatred of the drivers in front of me, and then an enthusiastic cursing of the day I was born.

These are feelings and actions that reflect a general unhappiness with the situation, but when I think it through, despite myself, I realize that my attitude isn't as valid as I want it to be. For one thing, it's my own fault I'm late; for another, I don't own the road and everyone else has a right to it as much as I do; I happen to like living in cities rather than the countryside, and that means other people and traffic; most importantly, without traffic lights, driving would be extremely dangerous for everyone. And because everyone together is more important than me and the appointment I'm late for, I need to grow up and change my attitude. For the record, however, I still have serious questions for the city planners who decide how red lights are timed.

This applies to bigger and more important things too. Perhaps someone's frustration isn't caused by traffic but because they want a house, or a car, or a spouse, that isn't theirs. Their desire conflicts with reality, and unfortunately for us, reality is bigger than we are and always wins. If happiness only means getting what we want, then we're in trouble and maybe happiness is impossible, and life is nothing more than frustration, and civilization is discontent, and hell is other people. Aristotle's book is all about how happiness is way more complex and interesting than that. Maybe it's good for us to not get what we want sometimes, and maybe the good of our community and the good of ourselves can overlap. Let's see where this goes.

Fr. Andy

Figure 2: Some guy

Precision: Not Rocket Science

"Precision is not to be sought for alike in all discussions." (I.3)

If you were on a trolley, asks a famous problem, and it was about to run over five people unless you pulled a lever, would you pull it? What if pulling the lever switched the trolley to a different track that would cause it to kill two people instead? What if one of those two people was a Nazi, or someone who drives slowly in the passing lane? What if the other person was a child, or Baby Yoda? What if pulling the lever caused you to be killed as well?

Examples like the Trolley Problem illustrate, among other things, the unbelievable complexity and weirdness that human life can potentially have. I'm not sure I know the answer to any but the simplest versions of the Trolley Problem, and I'm pretty relieved that, up to this point in my life, I've never been in that situation. I don't ever expect to be, and if I ever find myself on a trolley, I generally sit near the back to avoid having to make such a terrible choice.

Ethics, the study of human happiness, is not a very precise science precisely because of the complexity and particularity of human life illustrated by the Trolley Problem. In a very real way, it's impossible to know all the circumstances surrounding any given decision, which means there are times when knowing the right thing to do isn't a matter of applying clear and simple rules, but of figuring out what's best given the situation. This is called having the virtue of "prudence," which I'll talk about way later. The point I'm trying to make now is this: even if we can't get to absolute precision in writing detailed rules for conduct that will make us (and others) happiest in every possible situation, we can give good guidelines that are quite true, if not always as specific as we'd want them to be. In other words, this isn't rocket science, but it's not nothing.

It's worth noting that there are other ways to think about ethics. Deontology and utilitarianism are two important examples, and it's an interesting exercise to learn how and why they are different from the picture presented in this book. But there are tons of books that do that, and I don't want to make this book more boring than it already is. I'll present what I think is Aristotle's account, and let you figure out whether it makes sense to you.

Happiness: The Usual Suspects

> "[The many] think happiness is some plain and obvious thing, like pleasure, wealth, or honor." (I.4)

A good step toward finding the truth is to figure out what's false. So if we're looking for what happiness is, broadly speaking, we can get part of the way there by figuring out what it's *not*, and why. Aristotle sees three possible rivals to what he eventually claims happiness to be. They are: pleasure, wealth, and honor.

There's no doubt that feeling good feels good, but Aristotle distinguishes happiness from pleasure. Pleasure is (at least in this part of the book) a word he uses to describe some bodily enjoyment, like sex or eating fries. Happiness can and often does include bodily pleasure, but the two aren't the same, for reasons we'll get to soon. The reason he rejects pleasure as the whole of happiness is that there's more to human beings than our bodies, and if orgasms and tasting salt were the best thing in our lives, we'd be living the same lives as rats (or "fatted cattle" in Aristotle's book), which, for Aristotle at least, doesn't sound quite right.

Having money also feels pretty good, both because it feels secure to have it and because it can buy you other stuff that feels good. But again, wealth isn't the same thing as happiness. If you want evidence of this, just notice that rich people are either constantly seeking more money or so bored that they desperately seek out a pet project or drug to spend their time on. If money made them happy, they wouldn't need more of it, and they wouldn't need Instagram or seventeen dogs or cocaine. In any case, money is only worth anything when you trade it for something else, and happiness seems to be something you'd want to keep.

We don't talk much about "honor" these days; maybe "popularity" or "fame" would fit better with the way we think. This includes everything from being liked by your friends to winning an Oscar to having a building at Stanford named after you. All that sounds fine I guess, and sometimes you need to do really good things in order to be honored, but again there's something off. Honor depends on other people, and their perception of you, and that means they could be wrong. Plenty of jerks are popular and win awards and have buildings named after them. And even if people's perception is right, your honor is still dependent on them, and happiness seems like something you have yourself that can't be taken away because of an old tweet or someone else's mood changing.

Even worse, many times pleasure, money, and honor can act as distractions or drugs that we use to block out a deeper sadness that we don't want to face. The happy life, for Aristotle, is complete and doesn't need that kind of drug. Imagine sitting in your room and being happy just existing. That's closer to the kind of thing he's talking about when he says "happiness."

Figure 3: True love

The Meaning of Life

"Presumably, however, to say that happiness is the chief good seems a platitude, and a clearer account of what it is is still desired. This might perhaps be given, if we could first ascertain the function of man." (I.7)

Yes, dramatic section title. Sorry though, I'm not going to tell you the meaning of your life as an individual. I neither know nor care about that. But if we're the same species and have enough in common, there might be some meaning to being human, and so some meaning to human life. Aristotle thinks there is a purpose to human life, and he reasons that it has something to do with reasoning. But let's work our way there.

If you were to ask anybody besides the most stubborn philosopher what the purpose of an eyeball is, they'd say "to see," and if you asked them about the purpose of an ear, hand, or nosehair, they'd say "to hear," "to pick up fries," and "to repel the opposite sex," respectively. Similarly, if you asked what a banjo player is for, most people would say "banjo playing," and they'd say that "typing," "teaching," and "harassing homeless people" are the purposes of typists, teachers, and San Francisco police officers, respectively.

I could give more examples, and even different kinds of examples, such as the purposes of human inventions like chairs and golf clubs, but Aristotle's reasoning is that it would be very strange for *parts* of human beings to have a purpose, and *types* of human beings to have a purpose, but for human beings to have no purpose at all.

Sure, there are some things whose purpose is hard to understand, if they have one at all, like appendixes or tuna casseroles, but for a lot of things we can pick out a pattern: the purpose can be discovered by finding the thing it can do that other things can't—or at least can't do as well. Eyes can see, while ears and intestines can't. Banjo players can play banjo, while non-banjo players can't. So what's the thing that humans can do that other animals can't? Well, it could be any number of things. We can write bad poetry, build skyscrapers, misspell tattoos, etc. But, according to Aristotle, we can boil all of these other abilities down to one: *reasoning*.

One comment before I even explain what this means for Aristotle: it seems to be the case that some other animals can do something at least similar to reasoning. My cat, for example, seems to notice when I give her dry food when she prefers canned food, and expresses her frustration by knocking my coffee mug down in protest. I won't make a big fuss out of this here since it doesn't make much of a difference to the argument. The purpose of a banjo player is still playing the banjo even if other people can sort of play it too.

But what does it mean that our purpose, as human beings, is reasoning? Aristotle divides it into two aspects. Because the word for reasoning in Greek (*logos*) can mean "conversation," living a life of reason means living and interacting well with others. So part of what it means to be human, and part of fulfilling our purpose as human beings, is living a life of community—caring about others. The other part is just plain old thinking. The rest of the *Nicomachean Ethics* lays out all the details of these two aspects of reasoning.

The Definition of Happiness

"Activity of the soul in accordance with virtue." (I.7)

All this being said, it becomes clear that for Aristotle, happiness is an *activity* (whether social or intellectual) and not a passivity or possession—that is, happiness is something we *do*, not something done to us or something we have. This insight alone, I think, can clear up a lot of people's confusions. It can be toxic for people in friendships or romantic relationships to expect the other to "make them happy," as if happiness is something received passively. Similarly, it is confusing to think that happiness is something we *have*, as if it's a substance out there that can be moved from place to place or deep fried until golden brown. Happiness is, in a sense, something that we feel, but the feeling of happiness follows the activity, which is primary. This is something I'll return to at the end of this book.

That happiness is an activity *of the soul* is a little harder to understand. Aristotle did not believe that the soul was some separate entity apart from the body, as if the soul and body were two different beings. For him, a soul was a principle that makes a living thing live, and a human soul is a principle that makes a human to be alive as a human. So what he means by that phrase is that *happiness is an activity that human beings do because they are the kind of beings they are*, with the kinds of souls they have—in other words, "activity of the soul" is another way to say "rational activity," which for Aristotle very much involves the body. Plants and animals have souls, according to Aristotle. Plant souls allow them to grow and reproduce; animal souls allow them to sense things and move around. Aristotle's point here is that human happiness doesn't consist in the activities of plants or animals, which are only part of our lives, but in the activities particular to us as humans.

This is an important point: if people understood that reproduction and sensory activity weren't the greatest purposes of their lives, the club scene and pornography industry would lose a lot of money. Yes, these other activities are *part* of human life: eating, sleeping, reproducing, seeing, hearing, but Aristotle understands that a person can do all of these things and still be unhappy. Happiness is an activity, but not any of those activities, as necessary and pleasant as they often are.

Piecing things together, we come up with something a little weird. Happiness means two kinds of activity, corresponding to the two aspects of reasoning: *caring about others* and *thinking*. But this seems to go against experience. Isn't it possible to do both of those activities and still be unhappy? Aristotle adds some clarifications: we also need the basic essentials of life and some half-decent luck (not a mansion and supermodel wife, but a comfortable place to stay and a few good friends). But most importantly, happiness isn't just the activity of the soul, but the *virtuous* or *excellent* activity of the soul. So happiness isn't just caring and thinking, but doing them *really well*. And that last part is the hardest one, for a very particular reason.

Nothing More Than Feelings

> "There is found . . . also another element naturally opposed to the rational principle, which fights against and resists that principle." (I.13)

If you invented a device that allowed you to watch someone's inner turmoil, you'd get a blockbuster battle watching me wake up on any given morning. It would be easy if I were a morning person, and didn't stay up late watching *Daredevil* or writing unreadable books. It would also be easy if I could sleep in until noon every day the way God intended for us all. But no, I'm stuck living in the golden age of the Netflix series, which demands I stay up until 2 AM, as well as in the oppressive slavery of late capitalism, which requires me to wake up at an hour contrary to nature.

If you happen to be a morning person, plug in something else that you might struggle with. Maybe you like hamburgers but hear the voice of your doctor or trainer saying you should have a salad. Maybe you're angry at traffic but know you have no reason to be. Maybe you're attracted to another man but still love your husband. Aristotle would give a broad analysis of all these scenarios before getting into their particularities, and say that what is happening in all these cases is that there are two parts of your soul that are in conflict, and those parts he calls "reason" (which we've met before) and "the passions" (his term for "feelings" or "emotions").

Knowing what you *should* do and *wanting* to do it are two different things. Sometimes they're both there (I know I should spend some time reading every day, and I like doing it); sometimes they're not (I know I should wake up, but I don't want to—and all the other examples above). When you know what you should do but don't want to do it, that is, when reason and emotion are in conflict, sometimes reason wins and sometimes emotion wins. Aristotle calls it "virtue" when reason and emotion are both on the right side without conflict; it's "continence" when they're in conflict but reason wins out (like me getting up this morning); it's "incontinence" (yes, this also means peeing your pants) when emotion wins (like me eating Taco Bell yesterday); it's "vice" when both reason and emotion are on the wrong side (like someone with a harmful addiction or abusive relationship that they don't see as a problem). It seems to me that this whole way to analyze things reveals one of the most basic and universal realities of human life. I'll say a lot more about it in Book VII.

We can talk about this in another way, based on what we saw earlier. If Aristotle is right and happiness is "the virtuous activity of the soul," that means that being happy is acting in a reasonable way, and doing that well. What can get in the way of acting reasonably? Those emotions that pull us against what we know is best for ourselves (and other people, but more on that later). It's reasonable to respect other people's property, but sometimes we want what they have. This want creates a tension within us, and even if we can still act correctly (by not stealing from them), we struggle against ourselves to do this, which means we aren't doing it *well*. This struggle, in other words, makes us less happy.

The solution that is laid out in the rest of Aristotle's book is, to me, shockingly insightful and sophisticated, but I want to end this chapter with two very important concepts. First, it might be tempting to think that emotions themselves are the problem and that they should be cut out or ignored. If one side pulling us were simply omitted, the tension would go away. This is the farthest thing from Aristotle's mind, and even if it were possible, would amount to a mutilation of humanity, not a happy life. We can't just stop ourselves from feeling or pretend our feelings aren't there. Even trying to do that will do nothing but screw us up, and though he doesn't use words like "repression," Aristotle's entire account is an illustration of why this is in no way conducive to a happy life.

Emotions are a part of who we are, and trying to eradicate them is to harm ourselves and doesn't help in any way. But still, the tension is there and we should try to do something about it if we can. Aristotle's advice, laid out in the rest of the book, is about how to bring the emotions over to the side of reason. Sometimes this means persuasion (like talking ourselves into going to the gym); sometimes it means gradual habituation (like starting out with five push ups and slowly adding to them); sometimes it even means tough love (like making a rule that we don't get dessert if we didn't exercise that day). But it never means emotional amputation.

That means that step one is honesty. If we're feeling a certain way, and wanting things we know we shouldn't want, we need to admit it—at least to ourselves. Once that happens, then we can gain some benefit from the rest of Aristotle's ideas. But if we can't be honest enough with ourselves to admit what we're feeling, or do the work to figure it out in the first place, his book won't help us much. And I don't think anything else will either.

Figure 4: Me every morning

— Book II —

Learning

In This Chapter:

Habits, failures, toughing it out, assuming the worst about yourself.

Habits

> "Neither by nature, then, nor contrary to nature do the virtues arise
> in us; rather we are adapted by nature to receive them, and are made
> perfect by habit." (II.1)

The concept that is central to Book II is that of habits. I remember being a very miserable bully toward my little brother when we were younger. I'm not exactly sure what was up my butt, but for whatever reason I was really mean to him. During the same time, I remember feeling extremely guilty and sad for treating him so badly, and I remember promising myself over and over that I'd stop and be a better brother to him. But every time, it wouldn't take very long before I'd slip back into being a bully. This went on for years, and I remember really hating myself for not being able to change the way I treated him, and thinking I was just a monster, worse than anyone else for being the way I was.

The fact was that I had a deeply ingrained habit of letting my anger control the way I acted toward him, and habits have their own kind of force that needs to be dealt with in its own way. Changing a habit isn't like learning something new. I knew what I was doing was wrong and wanted to stop, but the knowledge didn't make the habit change. That's because habits aren't just intellectual things, the way knowledge and ignorance are. They also aren't just like emotions or moods, which come and go pretty quickly in the big scheme of things. My story with my brother illustrates this: my moods would fluctuate between anger and guilt, but the habit survived all those fluctuations.

Before I go on to describe how habits can change, it's worth going over a couple prerequisites. First, sometimes there are underlying issues that need to be dealt with on their own before the habits are faced. If your arm is injured, the wound needs to be tended to and healed before you start exercising it. In emotional things, this can happen in different ways, like therapy and self-discovery and stuff like that, but for whatever reason it's not something Aristotle spends much time discussing. But it is important, so figure out your crap. If you try to force things before you're ready, you'll just make it all worse. You shouldn't do pushups with an injured shoulder. Heal it first. This book isn't about emotional healing; it's about making gainz.

Second, remember that you're human, which means you have all kinds of limitations built into you. As of the writing of this sentence, I'm forty years old and feel like my knees are being amputated by two-pronged hipster-restaurant forks every time it rains outside. So I will never be a professional basketball player, no matter how hard I try or how much I practice. And that's fine, because I already make big-time philosophy money.

What I'm trying to say is that while building good habits is possible, our possibilities are limited by lots of things, from financial circumstances to family responsibilities to DNA, and our goal should be to do the absolute best we can while keeping our limitations in mind. On the other hand, what I just said can be used as a bad excuse if you're feeling lazy, so maybe forget I said it.

In any case, you should have a good idea of what you're working with. If you're the angry type by temperament or personality, that'll make it more of a challenge to gain the habit of patience. If you're particularly lusty, it'll take more effort to get temperate. But having a particular temperament or personality type is just the beginning of the story, not the end. And so on with the other virtues we'll talk about in the next chapter or two. But before we get into the particulars, let's see what all habits have in common.

Make Mistakes

"The virtues we get by first exercising them, as also happens in the case of the arts." (II.1)

Playing piano and physical fitness are both great illustrations of gaining a good habit. In both cases your particular circumstances need to be kept in mind—how much time you have to dedicate, your other responsibilities, your current abilities, whether you're tone deaf or have a bad shoulder, etc. On the other hand, the fundamental principle that brings about both is activity. In other words, if you want to be good at piano, sit your butt down and play, and if you want some muscle tone, get your flabby butt to the gym and move some weights around. You wouldn't wait until you magically knew piano before sitting down to practice. Nor would you wait until you were strong to start lifting weights. Why would you think you should wait until you're brave to ask your crush out for coffee? The principle is the same in all cases: the habit (piano, weight-lifting, or courage) comes about through action. You do it first, and then you have it. Don't wait until you have it first, because you'll be waiting forever.

It might seem backwards from a particular angle—how can I do brave things if I'm not brave? Or lift weights when I'm not strong? Or play piano when I don't know how? Well, anyone who's done these things (or done anything) will tell you to start somewhere, and wherever you're at is as good a place as any. But acknowledge where you're at. If you've never picked up a weight before, start light; if you've never sat down at a piano, don't jump into Rachmaninov. Not sure what to say about talking to your crush. Maybe say hi first before proposing marriage.

What happens when you start? You'll do badly. Which is fine. Laugh at yourself and try again. I find it interesting that while humility isn't something Aristotle would describe as a virtue, it seems to underpin a lot of his advice. In the case of gaining habits, perfectionism is poison. The word "perfect" in its roots means "complete," which means you won't have it when you start or while you're learning. Perfectionism can drive you to be as good as possible, but if you expect to have perfection before you've paid your dues by screwing up ten thousand times, you need a reality check. You'll either get way more frustrated than you need to, or you'll give up. Like I said, laugh at yourself and try again. Or, try guitar and pilates instead of piano and weight lifting.

A big part of what it means to try again is to understand what you did wrong before. That's why mistakes are such an important part, not only of learning, but of building habits. But here it's really important that the mistake doesn't become a part of your habit. That's why a lot of good instructors stress good form when they're teaching beginners. If your shoulders are in the wrong position during a bench press, you could really hurt yourself, and you certainly won't be progressing much. The same goes for using the wrong fingers when you start piano. This is why good teachers are important.

We Do Need Some Education

"It makes no small difference, then, whether we form habits of one kind or of another from our very youth; it makes a very great difference, or rather all the difference." (II.1)

I don't envy parents. Even aside from the obvious discomforts and annoyances like diapers and teenagers, I don't think I'd ever have the patience to take care of someone hour after hour and year after year. I can barely do that with myself. And even worse is the fact that there are so many ways to mess up. If you don't pay enough attention to them you could cause insecurity; if you pay too much attention to them they might become narcissists. I have no idea how to do it and I don't want to know. But my job here is to explain what I think Aristotle meant, and maybe he knew—after all, he had a son, and the book I'm talking about was dedicated to him.

Forming good habits in youth, which is Aristotle's definition of education, makes "all the difference." There's a lot going on here. For one thing, the education of the young is the most important thing, not only for an individual or a family, but also for the state, which according to him should be deeply involved in education. But education isn't limited to, or even mainly about, the transfer of knowledge or training for a job. Education is primarily about learning good habits.

What this fundamentally means for Aristotle is that young people should be taught how to feel the right way. This doesn't sound like something we'd like today, but it's still very much a part of our world. When a kid is given a gift, she's taught to say "thank you," not just because it's good to be polite, but because it's good to feel grateful when you're given a gift. And repeated actions like saying thank you can, as we'll see later, eventually affect the way we feel. When a kid is being a bully to others, the issue needs to be addressed because taking pleasure in causing pain to others is a bad way to feel—it's the *wrong* way to feel.

Feelings, for Aristotle, are not the entirety of someone's personality. They are, especially in youth, more like raw material that's available to be formed. The way this happens is through developing good habits, and the way that happens is through an environment where they are encouraged to feel the right way. This has two important aspects. One is negative—rules that regulate and discourage bad behavior and harmful feelings. The other is positive—rules that encourage enjoyment of good things.

The second one, encouraging kids to have fun doing good things, I've often seen neglected. Schools and parents often punish wrongdoing, but youthful exuberance is exhausting and it can be tempting to neglect joy for the sake of discipline. That, to Aristotle, is a very bad idea, and I think he'd be pretty horrified at the way a lot of our schools are run. Bland lectures seven hours a day and busy work when they get home don't teach kids to love learning—they teach them to get used to boredom. And that's a really crappy thing to do to a kid. I think we have a lot to learn from Aristotle on this point.

But what if you're old already? In other words, what if you had a bad upbringing and find yourself an adult with bad habits that have been there for years? Well, nobody had the perfect childhood, so we're all sort of in the same boat—maybe some in different parts of it than others. In fact, if it were too late to change your habits as an adult, there would be no point for Aristotle to have written this book, since it's addressed to adults and has the goal of helping them become better people. So maybe you have your work cut out for you when it comes to becoming a better (and therefore happier) person, but it's never too late.

Be Mean

> "It is no easy task to be good. For in everything it is no easy task to find the middle." (II.9)

I actually hate puns, but this one was too obvious. Aristotle's "golden mean" is pretty obvious too. It says that the virtuous act is in the middle between two extremes. Some examples are easy—don't eat too much or too little, but just the right amount. Other examples are confusing and kind of dumb. Should we commit adultery or murder in moderation? Should we be concerned about consuming too little cocaine? Can we love wisdom too much?

It's not really about the middle at all. If eating 300 pounds of food per day is too much and zero pounds is too little, that doesn't mean that 150 pounds is virtuous. All the golden mean means is the amount that's right depending on the circumstances. If you're a weight lifter, the right amount of food for you is way more than it would be for a ballerina. The right amount of adultery and murder is zero. So the mean is relative.

Relative doesn't mean meaningless though. When people say that something is "relative" they sometimes mean it's arbitrary. But relative doesn't mean that. It means "related to . . . ." The right amount to eat is related to your nutritional needs given your situation, and that's anything but arbitrary. This is a clear case where ethics has a pretty immediate bearing on happiness. Eat too much or too little, and you'll start hurting pretty quickly. Even if happiness is nothing other than pleasure, moderation is still a good idea.

You can plug your age, height, and body type into a website and it'll give you a fairly precise number of calories you should consume every day. Other things aren't so easy to figure out. What's the right amount of laughing you should do? You'd think the more the better until you try it at a funeral or when your friend tells you something tragic that happened to them that day. You'd quickly find yourself with fewer friends, and maybe none, and that will definitely affect your happiness.

As the laughter example illustrates, it's not just about some amount or quantity when it comes to virtue. It's about time and place, intensity, duration, manner. If you laugh at a joke too loudly at a restaurant and embarrass your date, it might be your last one with her. If you laugh too intensely or too long, you might turn them off by looking too desperate to gain their approval. There are similar delicacies in thinking about handshakes and hugs and drinking; there is a right amount to open up to someone you've known your whole life versus someone you met a week ago. There is even a "right" distance to stand from someone when you're talking to them.

Human society is full of subtle rules like this that we might not even notice until someone breaks them, and sometimes different societies have different sets of rules. All this doesn't mean that everything is arbitrary. It just means that it's relational—it's related to the situation and the society you're living in. And even if the particular rule is different in different societies, breaking the rule could leave you just as alone, and that's pretty lousy no matter where you are. So understanding and living according to the "mean" is important, even if it's complicated and dependent on merely social realities.

But wait: it gets worse. It's not just about delicacy in social situations so people don't think you're awkward. Awkwardness is very often just caused by simple ignorance or innocence. If you'd only known she had a crush on you, you'd have acted differently. But moderation is even more about your inner life, and the relationship between reason and emotion that we saw before. You rarely eat too much because you just don't know what the right amount is, as if new knowledge would fix everything. You eat too much (at least I do) because you *like* it. And you know you should stop with the fries, and you'll regret it tomorrow, but fries are so damned good that you need to eat every damned fry in the room. The same thing goes for sleeping, and drinking, and sex. The problem isn't ignorance. The problem is pleasure.

Pleasure and Pain

"We must take as a sign of states of character the pleasure or pain that supervenes upon acts." (II.2)

Have you ever seen somebody eat a three-pound corned beef sandwich on a dare or to win a contest or to commemorate my friend Mike's wedding which was happening the following day? It's quite a sight. In some ways, competitive eating is not only hilarious but impressive. It requires a great deal of willpower and self-control, especially after the first twenty minutes. That's because at some point it hurts, very badly. So badly you don't want to eat corned beef for several years afterward.

It's quite healthy to feel pain after eating way too much. It's also quite healthy to feel pleasure while eating the right amount. But pleasure and pain can be gauges of vice as well as health. When we watch an assassin in a movie, it's one thing when we watch him murder someone in cold blood. It's another when we see no guilt or sadness or any other pain in his eyes afterward, or even worse if we see pleasure. It isn't just the action of killing that illustrates something wrong in the assassin's soul, but the feeling or lack of feeling as well. Pleasure and pain are indicators of the condition or character of the person. What we like and dislike are deep reflections of who we are. That's why these are things we naturally discuss when we're trying to get to know someone. Even something as seemingly neutral as music can say a lot: when someone likes the same kind of music we do, it somehow tells us they feel things in a similar way.

Aristotle has a really weird description of pleasure. I'm not even sure he considers it a definition, or if he thinks pleasure can even have a definition (there are a handful of important words he doesn't think can be defined, like "actuality"). In any case, he describes pleasure as "something that accompanies acts," which is weird. Pleasure is something that's also kind of there when we do stuff. Even when we expand this idea, I'm not sure how helpful it is. Let's add to it: it's not just doing things that feels good, but having things done to us: playing piano is (sometimes) pleasant, but so is listening to someone else play piano. In the second case, we're not acting but receiving or passive. Or if listening is still too active for you, maybe a massage is a better example. But then again, doing things and having things done to us can also hurt, so pain needs to be part of this picture too. When we're not so good at piano, it hurts to have to play it; when the masseuse pushes too hard, it causes us pain. This goes right back to the golden mean stuff in the last section. When an activity is proportionate to us (whatever that means in the given situation), it feels good; when it's not, it feels bad. So let's say pleasure is something that accompanies action or passion done well, and pain is something that accompanies action or passion done badly. I guess it's one thing to eat a french fry and another thing to savor it. I still think this is pretty mysterious, but that's all I'll say about it for now.

Ok, one more thing. Pain and pleasure can make the act itself better or worse. I'm told that people sometimes walk around just for fun. It seems strange to me, but who am I to judge? But if they had hurt their back earlier that day, the activity of walking would not only be less pleasant, but less of a walk—they'd be limping maybe, or need a cane, or walk less. Similarly, there's an easy way to tell a great singer from a good one. It's not that the great singer hits the notes more precisely. It's that she has fun while she sings. This is why pleasure and pain are so important for virtue. The "continent" person is the one who wants to go to the strip club but doesn't—he would take pleasure in it if he went, which shows something about his conflicted character. The virtuous one doesn't want to go at all, and if he were dragged there, he'd hate it.

Bendy McStickerson

"We must drag ourselves away to the contrary extreme; for we shall get into the intermediate state by drawing well away from error, as people do in straightening sticks that are bent." (II.9)

So there's a lot to figure out when it comes to doing the right thing, the thing that will make you happiest in the long run. Many of the virtues that we'll talk about in the next few chapters have to do with social life, which is pretty complicated. But even besides the complexity, there are forces called feelings, not directly in our control, that push and pull us away from the middle. Ignoring them or pretending they aren't there doesn't help at all. If anything, when we ignore how we feel we're just hiding the true causes of our actions from ourselves. This whole situation is like trying to throw a perfect pitch in a hurricane. That's why virtue is so impressive, and so rare.

And yet Aristotle wrote this book so we could do exactly that, so he doesn't think it's impossible, and neither do I (as far as I am from it). But getting there takes a lot of practice. In the meantime, he has a bit of advice for us noobs: play it safe. When it's difficult to hit the middle, much of the time that's because there's an emotion or desire pulling us more in one direction than another, and it throws off our balance. In these cases, Aristotle advises us to lean back in the other direction to balance things out.

This is especially the case with pleasure, about which, in Aristotle's words, we are not impartial judges. Most of us, most of the time, tend to want more than is good for us when pleasure is involved. That's why I'm not capable of eating just a few fries. Maybe your thing isn't fries, but it's probably something, whether Skittles or sex or sleep or something else. And maybe you've got more control over it than I do with fries, but you might still overindulge in one way or another.

In any case, when a stick is bent in one direction, Aristotle advises bending it the opposite way, not just straightening it. The idea is not just balance, but detachment. We're usually too attached to pleasure to make good judgments about it, and it can often get us into trouble. Denying ourselves is a way to clear our heads and gain some freedom from that kind of pressure, at least over time. This kind of delayed gratification is central to Aristotle's advice, and makes a big difference in our lives in the long run. At least I'm hoping so. Until then, I try to avoid ordering fries at all. I feel better about myself afterward, but in the moment I'm stuck with the worst thing of all: potato salad, the overindulgence of which is in no way tempting.

Figure 5: Bendy McStickerson

— Book III —

Virtue

In This Chapter:

Choices, non-choices, thinking well, bravery, keeping it in your pants.

What's Your Fault

> "Those things, then, are thought involuntary, which take place by force
> or by reason of ignorance." (III.1)

Some things aren't your fault at all, like someone else not noticing the stop sign and hitting your car with his. Some things are entirely your fault, like your calm, deliberate choice to punch him in the face after you both got out of your cars. Some things are in between, and sort of your fault, like when you cussed right after the guy hit your car with his.

Aristotle gives an account of what we might call "free will," but it's argued in practical terms, not metaphysical ones. Whether or not your choices are pre-determined by your genes and upbringing and the particular situation you're in and the little neurons firing in your little brain and God, you will be the one dealing with the consequences of your choices, not your genes or your upbringing or your circumstances or God. If you think you really had no choice and what you did wasn't your fault and therefore it's unfair for you to have consequences, I think Aristotle would politely invite you to form your own country with laws reflecting your beliefs, and wish you the best of luck. Whether or not there really is free will, we have to live like there is.

On the one hand, it's a pretty slippery slope to give people a blank check of excuses for their actions. If the thief shouldn't be punished because he had a bad upbringing and couldn't help it, why not the racist for the same reasons? If you couldn't stop yourself from cussing your friend out because he made you so angry, maybe the adulterer can't stop his affair because his secretary is too attractive. This train of thought gets pretty silly pretty fast.

On the other hand, not taking any account of circumstances at all doesn't seem fair either. It really is a different thing when a clear-thinking adult commits a crime versus a teenager who has been abused his whole life. Sometimes mercy really is the right thing. This whole story goes back to how complex and sometimes imprecise ethics can be, because it's all in the details.

Aristotle does give some tools to deal with culpability (how much something is your fault). Things done in total ignorance or completely by force are not your fault at all. If you really didn't know anyone else was in the car when you farted, it's fair game. If someone had a gun to your head and forced you to hurt a fluffy kitten, it's their fault, not yours. Some scenarios are absolute, like when you really had no way to know someone else was in the car or if there really was a gun to your head. Sometimes it's kind of your fault, like when you could have known something pretty easily, or had some way to escape without hurting the kitten.

It's in this last category that we can put actions that come about through the force of passion. If you're in a fury and in the midst of your anger you raise your voice and say hurtful things unfairly, to some degree your anger "made" you do what you did. On the other hand, you could still have said nothing, or walked away, or not gotten into the argument in the first place, so you're not entirely innocent. The comparison between passion and alcohol can be useful here. When you're drunk you do things you wouldn't do sober, but you're still the one who chose to drink that much. In the worst scenario, you might not be guilty of pre-meditated murder, but you are guilty of manslaughter.

So we can vaguely summarize by saying that there's a kind of spectrum working here, and that there's a range of free will and degrees of freedom working in everyday life. Some things aren't our fault at all, namely things done in total ignorance or completely by force; some things are completely our fault with zero gray area, namely things that are deliberated and chosen. All the rest falls in between, where our choices are to some degree affected by some passion or another. But most of these choices are still our fault, because to some degree our passions follow from our character, which is to some degree our responsibility (more on this below). Sorry for the vagueness, but again, we're doing ethics, not math.

What Not to Deliberate

"Now about eternal things no one deliberates; e.g., about the material universe or the incommensurability of the diagonal and the side of a square." (III.3)

There's a lot of stuff out there to think about, but sometimes we waste our thoughts on stuff that isn't worth it. When someone hurts us, we can spend hours or days or years obsessing and re-living the moment—we can take a moment that hurt and make it hurt for way longer. I know I've done this, and most of the time it's not by choice or even something I notice doing. But whether it's by choice or not, most of the time it's a waste of time. Thinking about what happened in the past just for the sake of doing it isn't going to change what happened, and obsessing about it for years won't make you feel any better. There might be a processing time where thinking about it is important just to understand what happened and how you feel about it, but a point comes where we do more damage to ourselves than the person who hurt us.

Another waste of time is getting frustrated with realities we can't change. The fact is, there's traffic on the road that I need to be on during a time that I need to be on it. My anger won't make the traffic go away, any more than it will make pi a rational number. More likely than not, the traffic was caused by somebody doing something stupid, but that stupid event stupidly happened in the past, and my frustration can't change it now. You might disagree with me on this, but I feel the same way about people who get angry at God. Whether or not there is a God, I doubt he owes you anything, or becomes sad if you get mad at him, as if God has low self-esteem. And I really doubt your frustration will change his mind about anything, any more than it will change the traffic or the value of pi. Yes, traffic, God, and the value of pi are all very different things, but one thing they have in common is that they don't change when you get mad and obsess over them. In cases like this, it's best to accept reality (whatever it might be) and move on to the next thing to think about.

Other things are worth spending time thinking about. One form of thinking is what Aristotle calls "deliberation," which is what we do when we try to figure out the best way to get what we want (or, more precisely, what we should want). For example: let's say I want cowboy boots (don't ask why—there is no answer). There are many ways to get to this goal: I could shop online or go to the local cowboy boot store (apparently there is such a thing). But there are many brands and styles, so I'd need to do research. Are they supposed to fit perfectly right away or be slightly tight and break in? What are the pros and cons of the different materials they can be made from? There are different ways I can research as well—YouTube reviews, websites, asking people. Then I remember my cousin used to work at one of those cowboy boot stores, so I could ask him, etc. etc.

This is to illustrate, among other things, that deliberation can often become overwhelming, precisely because there can be so many options to get to your goal, and finding the best among them is often difficult. But even "best" can mean different things—it can mean best quality, for example, but that rarely coincides with best price. One way to trim the fat when it comes to complex decisions like this is to let reality trim it for you. There is a certain amount of money I have to work with, so that omits half my cowboy boot options right there. This isn't something to mourn, but to celebrate—half my deliberation was done for me by my bank account. I also wear black a lot (both because I'm a priest and because I'm goth), so a lot of options are omitted due to color. After that, it was pretty easy to figure out the cowboy boots that were right for me. They arrived today in the mail, and my life will never be the same.

This, like all my examples, is a stupid example. It does illustrate some aspects of deliberation, but ethical and social decisions are much more difficult and complicated. Where to go to college, whom to marry, how to deal with a difficult friend, whether to move to a new city, are each a very different story than cowboy boots. In general, though, the same pattern can apply: lay out your options, let your circumstances narrow your options down, and then see what makes sense when everything is balanced. Many times, several options are just fine, which means your job is to just pick one. Hamlet famously and annoyingly spent way too much time thinking and deliberating, and we all know what happened to him (or should know—if not, put this book down now and go read *Hamlet*). Deliberation is also something that needs moderation. At some point you need to figure your crap out and just pick.

Two final points about deliberation for now: first, deliberation is about *how* to do the right thing or best thing, not *whether*. If you know what you should do without any doubt, your deliberation is done. It's a confusing mess of a waste of time to deliberate whether you should do something you already know you should do. Second: Aristotle makes a cool point that the last thing you think about is the first thing you do ("the end of deliberation is the beginning of action"). In other words, work backwards. You want to write a book. That's your final goal. In order to have the book, you need each chapter. In order to have chapters, you should have an outline. In order to have an outline, you need to write it down. In order to write it down, you need to open your laptop. That last thing you thought about is the first thing you do. Now open your laptop and get to work.

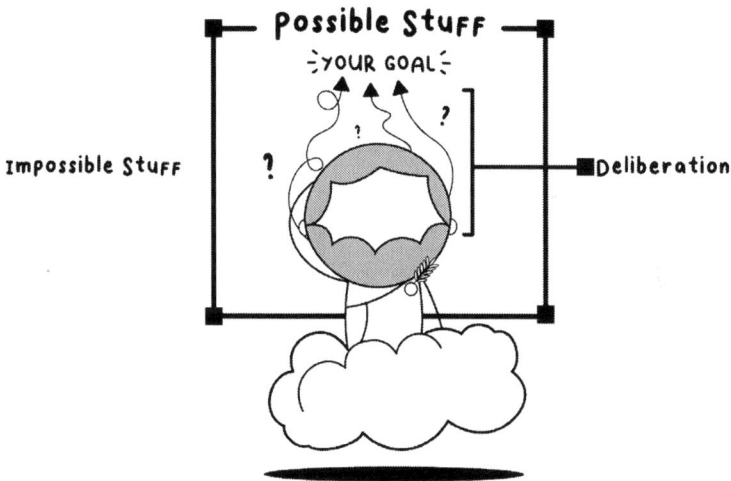

Figure 6: What to deliberate

Clear Eyes

"Each state of character has its own ideas of the noble and the pleasant, and perhaps the good man differs from others most by seeing the truth in each class of things, being as it were the norm and measure of them." (III.4)

Let's say you're watching a movie for the first time. But as you drive to the theater, your date tells you that their ex (whom you hate) just saw it and absolutely loved it. This distracts you enough that you forget to buy popcorn when you get to the theater, which in turn causes your blood sugar to drop during the movie. The facts that you chose the stickiest spot in the theater to sit, and that the guy in front of you is somehow nine feet tall, make matters worse. None of this means you'll hate the movie, of course, but there's a chance that you won't like it as much as you would have had none of these things happened. Whereas you might have rated the movie an 8, it might now be a 6 in your judgment.

Our judgment, in other words, can often be affected by our mood. But if our moods are habitual, that means they could affect our judgment all the time. This might actually help explain the different tastes that people have in things—and if so, it might be humbling to think about. Maybe you like the bands you like not because they make better music, but for more arbitrary reasons.

With a lot of things, taste isn't really a big deal. If someone prefers fish to steak for dinner, I don't really think that says anything about their character. Or if they like Stone Temple Pilots more than Nirvana. Even things that are more difficult to understand, such as enjoying country music, or ketchup on a hot dog, are mostly harmless. But somewhere—and it's kind of blurry where this line is—things change when it comes to taste. If someone has a taste for violence—if they take joy in bringing others pain—it's not a harmless subjective thing to be written off; there's something wrong going on inside them. If someone has sexual attraction to children, this is not a matter for personal preference, it is a serious issue. Whether we categorize these things as disorders or crimes or anything else, they aren't just matters of taste.

The examples don't have to be as extreme as violence or pedophilia either. Like I said, there is a gray area, but it does gradually become a darker gray. Perhaps someone doesn't take joy in bringing others pain, but they spend the majority of their time playing extremely violent video games. They aren't hurting others in this case, but they are kind of wasting their lives. Maybe someone doesn't exactly enjoy self-harm, but they have a taste in food that is particularly unhealthy and refuse to eat anything else. This isn't an immediately destructive thing, but it will catch up to them eventually.

Food, as usual, is a good example. No matter what your taste in food is, healthy is healthy. It doesn't matter if, like me, you love cheeseburgers and despise salads. That preference has nothing to do with the reality that one is good for you and the other isn't. That "bad" taste isn't going to kill me immediately—it's (usually) not going to affect me like eating poison would—but it is bad for me. Aristotle would expand this to a lot of different aspects of life, and say that education really means developing a taste for things that are good for you in all parts of life. The virtuous person would like healthy foods, healthy relationships, healthy music, healthy activities, healthy games, whatever any of these things might be.

In fact, what it really *means* to be a virtuous person for Aristotle is to habitually have this kind of taste for healthy things, and to see unhealthy things as repulsive. And conversely, you can tell a bad or vicious person by their vision as well. When someone sees a bad thing as if it's a good thing, that means there's something unhealthy going on in their eyes, like if someone looks at a white piece of paper and sees yellow because of the jaundiced fluid in their eyeball. The point of Aristotle's ethics is to help us go from bad taste and bad vision to good taste and clear vision—to like and enjoy only what's actually good for us.

You Can Do It

> "But perhaps a man is the kind of man not to take care. Still they are themselves by their slack lives responsible for becoming men of that kind." (III.5)

This is where things can get very discouraging. The fact is, many of us really like things that are bad for us objectively, whether it's a food or an activity or a relationship. Sometimes we don't even know it's bad for us, and this can be due to either ignorance or vice—maybe I don't know that cheeseburgers are bad for me because I've simply never been taught it, and maybe I don't know they're bad for me because I don't want to know, because I like them too much.

So it seems like we're stuck. We wake up one day and realize we've got some rotten habits that mess up our lives, and yet they are strong habits that are hard, or sometimes seemingly impossible, to break. Somehow it doesn't even seem fair. How is it your fault that you happen to have a sweet tooth? And yet sweet food can be harmful when you eat too much of it, which, unfortunately, is exactly the amount you need to satisfy your craving. How is it your fault that your friends and family cussed like sailors when you were growing up, and now you have a habit of it, which makes your life as a parish priest particularly complicated?

Whether it's "nature" (something built into your DNA, like a sweet tooth) or "nurture" (like being brought up in a cussy culture), we don't really have a choice of what we're given to work with when it comes to living well. Some people have genetic gifts that others don't, and some people were brought up with better habits than others. That sucks and isn't really our fault, but there's no changing the past. What we can do, though, is make the best of the cards that we've been dealt. And if you ask me, the people who do well with bad cards are the real heroes. I don't think getting super rich when you started out with a million-dollar loan from your dad is very impressive.

And Aristotle does assume that you can do something with the cards you were given. If you're of the opinion that your genes and your past make you who you are, and you can't do anything about it at all, you don't need to bother with the rest of this book—though I doubt you'd have picked it up in the first place if you believed that. I think Aristotle would go even further and say that, to some degree, even the character you have right now is partially your own doing already, and some of the cards you have right now are already your fault. You might not have chosen to have a sweet tooth, but every time you overdid it with the Twinkies was your choice and nobody else's, so even if the sweet tooth wasn't your fault, the extra chubb on your belly is. In a sense, the stuff we inherit genetically and culturally is more like raw material than it is a completed human being, and what we do with it makes a bigger difference in who we are than what we are given. To me, evidence of this is identical twins who were raised in the same home, but who turned out very differently. They have the same genes and a very similar upbringing, and yet came up with a different result with the same raw material.

When I say that even your character is partially your own fault because of the choices you've already made, that is meant to be a very hopeful idea, because it is. If your previous choices made you the miserable jerk you are today, that means your current choices can just as definitely make you into a more amenable jerk in the future. Just remember to be patient. It took twenty years of nose-picking or raising your voice or eating too many Twinkies (i.e., one) to get you to where you're at today—thousands of individual choices and actions. It'll take a lot of time and many choices to turn the tide. But just like one choice at a time made the bad habits as strong as they are now, one choice at a time can change them. And they'll change very gradually: first (and maybe for a long time) you'll have to force yourself one choice at a time; then it'll get easier by small increments; at some point it won't be so painful; some day, you might even enjoy doing the right thing. Again, this applies to exercise, or playing piano, or courage and temperance and all the other virtues we'll talk about later.

In some cases the habit is so strong and your feelings are so off-kilter that your vision is impaired in the way I described in the last section: you're so into nose-picking or screaming or Twinkies that you no longer even understand why it's wrong other than other people telling you it is. This is where friendship, trust, faith, and mentorship become very important. Sometimes you don't see things with your own eyes because of the damage they've sustained, but others can lead you gradually to heal and transform until you can begin to see and feel the truth yourself. In fact, that is exactly the role of friendship and community, according to Aristotle. I'll say more about transforming habits and the role of friendship later.

Courage

"Courage is a mean with regard to feelings of fear and confidence." (III.6)

Now that we're almost a third of the way through the book Aristotle finally gets around to talking about an actual virtue, and it turns out to be courage. For him, the best example of courage is a soldier. In fact, he seems to say that the courage of the soldier is the only real courage there is, and everything else we call courage is kind of a watered-down imitation. That actually seems right to me, but it doesn't really matter for the purposes of this book. Very few of us (hopefully) will ever have to fight in a war, and what he says of the watered-down versions of courage applies just as well to actual courage too.

So let's look at a more everyday example. You're interested in someone romantically but are afraid to tell them. What exactly are you afraid of in this scenario? Being precise (and honest) about the object of your fear can be important in understanding what's going on and facing it. Saying you're afraid of rejection is probably right, and it might be even more specific in your mind—maybe you're afraid she'll point and laugh in your face and have her friends point and laugh at you too, until you pee your pants and run away, but they run after you, pointing and laughing the whole time, calling you Awkward Flirty Peepants for the rest of your life. We've all been there.

Then again, maybe that won't happen at all. But your fear is stopping you from actually talking to her. It's especially annoying when you see others asking people out all the time with heroic confidence, and you wonder if they're just born with it and you'll never have it, and you're just destined to die alone, soaked in your own urine.

It might be the case that some people are just naturally more confident than others, but in my experience people become confident at things that they've done a lot. Confidence and courage, just like any virtue, aren't external substances that you have or don't have, as if you can add or subtract them by the gallon. They are habits, which means they increase by practice. In fact, an important aspect of courage is that it's realistic. The courageous soldier isn't the one who pretends there's no danger. He's the one who knows exactly what the danger is and acts well anyway. So being confident doesn't mean pretending you're not afraid.

What does it mean? Well, just like any habit, gaining it has to start somewhere. Maybe you're not ready to ask her out, so perhaps saying hi is a good start. In fact, if you haven't ever said hi to her before, maybe do that before you continue daydreaming about dates.

On the other hand, I don't know a damn thing about dating, so let's try a different example. Most people are afraid of public speaking (about 75 percent, according to the one second of research I just did on Google). I can testify that you can become a good public speaker even if you start off not only shy but terrified of it. And the way to do it is, like I've said over and over again, practicing as much as possible and learning from your mistakes. After a while (I don't think you can calculate exactly how long), you'll find yourself less nervous.

The thing is, you'll be confident in this because you know there isn't much to be afraid of anymore, but that just means you learned the virtue of public speaking, not courage. You'll learn courage by doing that whole thing over and over again with every scary thing—thinking through your fear, determining the best course of action despite it, and doing what's right, not what's less scary. I think maybe that's one of the reasons why, of all the virtues, Aristotle talked about courage first: you kind of need it when you're learning any of them, because when you're learning them, they're new, which means they're scary.

Temperance

"The temperate man is so called because he is not pained at the absence of what is pleasant and at his abstinence from it." (III.11)

Later followers of Aristotle broadly divided emotions into two types, which they called "concupiscible" and "irascible." Irascible emotions generally had to do with the difficulties of life and all the obstacles we face when trying to get what we want (the short list is: hope, despair, fear, daring, and anger). Concupiscible emotions, on the other hand, just have to do with things we want or don't want, without reference to how difficult it is to get them (they're usually listed as: love, desire, joy, hatred, aversion, and sorrow). I'm not going to say much more about this division, and it's not really that important for my point right now except to say that, generally speaking, courage seems to be a virtue that moderates an irascible passion (namely fear) whereas temperance, then next one he talks about, moderates the principle and boss of all concupiscible passions, bodily pleasure.

Whereas fear pushes us away, pleasure pulls us in. As usual, you can use any example you want in order to understand what Aristotle is saying: the pleasure of eating french fries, the pleasure of avenging your father's death, the pleasure of watching a sunset. However, the virtue of temperance isn't equally important in all these different cases. That's because lots of the things we take pleasure in aren't really so addicting that they can harm or screw up our lives, which means they don't really need much effort to moderate. You don't really see people living on the streets because of their addiction to sunsets or the smell of orange blossoms.

When specifying which pleasures need to be moderated by the virtue of temperance, he boils it down to two: eating and sex. He gets even more specific and seems to be more concerned about sex than eating, but instead of being more specific, I'll actually add to his list. I think temperance should also be concerned with moderating alcohol and drugs, and other things like the amount of time we spend watching Netflix and playing video games. I'm adding to his list because I've noticed all these things become directly or indirectly harmful to people's lives, and therefore detract from their happiness.

Still, though, Aristotle does have a point when he focuses on the pleasure of sex. It's not only about its intensity or its ability to bring about life, but also about its ability to destroy. You don't even have to include acts of terrible violence like rape or child abuse in this, since those are as much about power and pain as they are about pleasure. Just think about how easily sexual desire can destroy marriages through adultery, or how quickly it can breed obsession, or cause someone to allow themselves to be hurt or disrespected, or, in all these cases and more, how it can cloud the mind. Sex (and sexual activity in general) seems to have the tendency to take over all of life like a tyrant. I don't think it's love that is blind, or even blinding, but lust. And if something clouds the mind that easily, by definition it can be irrational, and take away the happiness that is defined as rational activity.

Of course, that's not to say that the desire is itself bad, but only that it needs to be moderated. Whether or not you believe that sex should be reserved for marriage, it should be reserved in one way or another, and it, like everything else we do, should be guided by reason. By the way, if you're unconvinced about how dangerous sex can be, try giving it up for a while. If you find it difficult, it might have more power over you than you think. Then, if you're convinced of its power and want to learn the virtue of temperance, practice.

Book IV

Social Virtues

In This Chapter:

Cheap bastards, self-esteem, anger, laughter.

Generosity

> "It not easy for the generous man to be rich, since he is not apt either at taking or at keeping, but at giving away, and does not value wealth for its own sake but as a means to giving." (IV.1)

Temperance and courage, which we talked about in the last chapter, can have private expressions, at least to some degree: you can exercise moderation in eating even while you're alone, and you can be brave while walking through a dark hallway in your house even after everyone's fallen asleep. But in the first section of this book I mentioned how the community we live in is a more important thing than any individual for Aristotle, and that means that temperance and courage find their fullest expression in the midst of our social lives. On a small scale, social life requires self-control and bravery of some kind on a daily basis. On a larger scale, no society could exist without the basic respect for other people's property; nor could any country remain a country for long without the true courage of its soldiers.

The virtues described in Book IV seem to follow this trajectory even more, to the point where some might not seem to have anything besides a social aspect. This is just as it should be, since for Aristotle, social life is a quintessentially human thing. That being the case, and human society being tied, for better or worse, to money, we begin with the virtues that govern the proper use of money. There are, in fact, two of them: one for everyone, and one reserved just for rich people.

Generosity, the first of these, is the mean between two opposite extremes, but like many virtues, it is more contrary to one of the extremes than another. Let's call the two extremes "being wasteful" and "being a cheap bastard," respectively. For various reasons, Aristotle believes that generosity is more similar to being wasteful than it is to being a cheap bastard. For one thing, the virtue of generosity has to do with giving, and being wasteful is a vice because it means giving too much, or somehow or another in the wrong way. On the other hand, being a cheap bastard doesn't have to do with giving at all, but rather taking and keeping. This is not only a different kind of activity than giving, but it's also more difficult to "cure" (and being a cheap bastard, like all vices, is a kind of sickness). Aristotle observes that it's easier to teach someone to give with moderation when they give too much, than it is to teach someone who is stingy to give at all, which seems quite true in my experiences fundraising (though I'm not sure I've ever met someone who gives too much). The idea is that the cheap bastard loves money more than he loves people (which is why he is referred to as a cheap bastard), while the wasteful guy loves people more than money, as he should, but he doesn't do it in a balanced way.

Like any virtue, generosity is something that is relative to the individual. Just like a temperate amount of eating is based on someone's size and lifestyle, a generous amount of giving is based on someone's actual wealth, and what's generous for one person would be foolhardy or cheap for another. If I tried to give as much as some of the benefactors of the seminary, I'd be in so much debt that I couldn't pay it off in ten lifetimes. On the other hand, if Jeff Bezos donated exactly as much as I do to charity, he'd be as cheap a bastard as ever lived (which I think he might actually be).

Of course, it's not really the virtue of generosity if you give with bad or mixed intentions: if you donate to charity to write it off on your taxes, that's not a bad thing, and it might be an expression of the virtue of prudence, but it's not generosity. The same goes for buying someone dinner in hopes they'll give you a job, or buying a round at the pub so that people will like you, or giving good Christmas gifts so that people remember and give you good ones next year. None of those things are bad, but they aren't generosity because their goal is something other than giving itself. Remember that the real litmus test of virtue is pleasure: the generous person takes pleasure simply in the act of giving, and doesn't need any other motivation.

It's in this chapter, around halfway through his book on ethics, that Aristotle gets around to mentioning that stealing is wrong. But his reasoning for why it's wrong isn't the typical story we heard from our parents or teachers. Stealing, for Aristotle, isn't just wrong because it hurts others who lost the stuff we stole from them. It's fundamentally wrong because it hurts *us*. Yes, the 7-Eleven next to the White Castle in Troy, Michigan lost a Snickers bar or two some time around 1987, but I lost more: I became a thief. The vice, which expressed a fondness for gain greater than my respect for others, was more harmful than the loss of property. At the very least, we can say that lack of generosity in general makes me unhappy because it hurts my community, which is in some way a part of me as I am a part of it. And so with all the virtues in this book.

Magnificence

> "The magnificent man is like an artist; for he can see what is fitting and spend large sums tastefully." (IV.2)

The next virtue, which is dramatically called "magnificence," is similar to generosity, in that it involves giving money or material things. But there are two related reasons why generosity and magnificence are different. First, magnificence is more expensive and requires the giver to be quite wealthy. But that can't be the only difference, since that's just a difference of degree, and for Aristotle, you don't distinguish different kinds of things simply by "more" or "less." The more important difference is that the recipient of magnificence isn't an individual, or even a large group of individuals, it's a community. This is an important distinction, especially for Aristotle: a community is an organized, even organic, whole, not just a number of people in the same geographic location. So magnificence is generosity given to this organized whole we call a community (or city, or state, or country). But because it's a gift given to a larger entity, it costs more, which is really a secondary, though unavoidable, issue.

So it's one thing to generously help out a person in need: this is an important activity in a world where all of us find ourselves in need of one kind or another at some point in life. But it's another thing to help out an entire community. Buying someone a drink, or even buying a round for the whole pub, is a generous act. But building a hospital for a city is beyond generous, not only because it's more expensive, but because it's for a community, not an individual. Just as importantly, it's also for posterity. The round of beers comes and goes like a passing wind, or, more precisely, like a wave in the ocean. But the hospital remains (hopefully) for generations. The community it serves isn't just horizontal, in geographic space right now, but vertical through time. This largeness of scope seems to me to justify the name of the virtue magnificence.

Aristotle names different kinds of acts of magnificence (which at some point were given the name *liturgeia*, "acts for the people"), which he broadly organizes into works of necessity and works of beauty. This is worth reflecting on: Aristotle's notion of community and its needs is expansive, not minimalistic. We as a community need more than just the basic necessities, and those who provide for either of them are expressing the virtue of magnificence, but especially those who provide beautiful things. So it's one thing to build a hospital or library—it's a great and virtuous act for your whole community. But it's even better to build them well, and make them nice to look at. Not everyone goes to the hospital or library, but everyone passes by them, and when there are beautiful things to look at, it makes us love our city, and loving our city is a great thing to encourage—a beautiful thing.

The basic idea here is challenging, as are all the virtues. If you are a person with wealth, it is your duty to your community to use your wealth for the community's good, and to do so gladly and lavishly. To fail at this is not to be morally neutral but vicious. You are connected to your community for better or worse, and you have the power to make it better. And remember, this is about actual *giving*, not building a stadium that will ultimately bring you profit. Losing actual money in a permanent way is a prerequisite for this virtue. Otherwise you're just starting another business.

Doing this well requires good taste, which requires thoughtfulness and contemplation. What would really help your community? What are its needs, both in terms of necessity and in terms of beauty? Does it need another stadium, or would a park be better? We can even be more expansive in our application: you're building a skyscraper for your business; it won't make you any extra money to add some trim to the windows, or some fancy brickwork, but it will make the building look a lot nicer and improve the overall look of downtown. Do it. We don't need any more plain rectangular monstrosities in our cities.

This last idea allows for anyone, not just the super wealthy, to participate in magnificence in their own way. This is really what mowing your lawn or picking up litter is about. It's an act that you can do as an individual that helps your neighborhood as a whole look nicer. It's one good reason to build houses that look attractive from the outside: it's not just about showing off, it's about contributing to the beauty of your community. In fact, the person living inside the house is the one who sees it the least. That simple act (and there are others, such as decorating for holidays) is a way to express your belonging to a community.

Being a cheap bastard (or, even worse, a rich cheap bastard) isn't the only vice opposite to magnificence though. Being gaudy and showy is another. Being gaudy is not about spending too much money, but about doing it badly or in the wrong way. The example Aristotle gives from history is the pyramids, which are enormous, expensive, gaudy tombs. He is more impressed by buildings dedicated to the gods than to oneself, especially oneself after death. But there are plenty of more recent examples of this kind of tackiness. I remember being annoyed about this when visiting Rome: most of the gorgeous churches there had their facades defaced by the pope who was reigning while they were built having his name carved on them in giant letters. We have similar issues in America with people plastering their name in giant gold letters on top of hotel towers.

Magnanimity

> "The man is thought to be magnanimous who thinks himself worthy
> of great things, being worthy of them; for he who does so beyond his
> deserts is a fool, but no virtuous man is foolish or silly." (IV.3)

Magnanimity might be the most interesting virtue Aristotle describes in this book, and it's something that I think people easily misunderstand—probably because it's a virtue not many people have. I've sometimes seen it translated as "pride," and there might be some accuracy to that since describing "humility" as a virtue wasn't something Aristotle directly did. However, the way we use the word "pride" today seems to correspond more closely to what Aristotle considered a vice, which was thinking *too* highly of yourself. So for this section, I'll stick with the word "magnanimity" (which means "greatness of soul") to name the virtue, "arrogance" to name the vice on the side of excess, and "undue humility" to name the vice on the side of deficiency.

Stated simply, magnanimity means being great and knowing it. But like courage, there are watered-down versions that apply to the rest of us who aren't superheroes. The way courage is seen most fully in soldiers risking their lives for a noble cause, but shared in a way by people speaking in public, magnanimity is seen fully in people who are "great" (whatever that might mean), but it can be shared in a way by everyone. And to me, the shared version really reveals what this virtue is about. Magnanimity is defined not simply by greatness but also by self-knowledge. This is why the vices that are its opposites are defined by lack of self-knowledge, not lack of greatness. Arrogance means thinking you're greater than you really are; undue humility means thinking you're less than you really are. The vices are defined by a disconnect between your own self-image and the reality of who you really are. That means the virtue is defined by *accurate self-knowledge*.

So perhaps the closest approximation of "magnanimity" we have today is what we'd call "self-esteem." The excess might resemble what we describe as a narcissist. The deficiency would correspond to low self-esteem. Put in these terms, it makes sense that Aristotle said that the deficiency is more common than the excess. There are certainly plenty of narcissists around, but my sense is that the majority of people think much too little of themselves. In either case, the vice is damaging to happiness: narcissists, living in their dream world where they are God's gift to everyone, are annoying and therefore lonely; those with undue humility are overly self-critical and therefore self-isolating, and therefore lonely. This social aspect is one of many consequences of these vices, and it has another side as well: narcissists don't only hurt themselves but others (if you've never worked for a narcissistic boss, count that as one of the best blessings of your life); those with low self-esteem don't only isolate themselves, they deny the people they live with the good things they could provide. And like the other virtues, thinking about magnanimity reminds us what we owe to the people we live with.

In a way, all good deeds can fall under this virtue, and Aristotle makes a point that someone who understands their own worth wouldn't ever harm someone else, "for to what end should he do disgraceful acts, he to whom nothing is great?" You shouldn't hurt others (or yourself) because you're too good to do that, and you deserve to live the way a good person lives. You should avoid toxic relationships, or obsession, or making your life revolve around someone else, because nobody is worth what that does to you. You should forgive those who have wronged you because it is small-souled and petty to hold on forever to something done in the past, and it's a waste of your time and energy. You shouldn't whine and complain about what you don't have, because whatever it is you don't have isn't nearly worth what you are, and you have yourself. I find this analysis of morality much more attractive than giving guilt trips, though, as a Catholic, I understand the need for both (see the last section of this chapter, on shame).

Just like most of these virtues and vices, your upbringing and genetics and social factors have a big contribution to whether or not you have a habit of magnanimity. Low self-esteem especially is a reality that can be the consequence of many things outside your control—and it's worth noting here that when Aristotle calls something a "vice," it simply means any bad habit that is harmful to your life in any way, not necessarily something entirely your fault. For example, I remember (vaguely—it was a long time ago) beginning kindergarten not really knowing any English besides a few words I'd learned from *Sesame Street*. There wasn't much ESL available in those days, especially when your first language was Chaldean, and I was therefore left to my own, very limited, devices. So I remember day after day sitting in class an utterly bewildered five-year-old kid, watching a friendly lady make noises I didn't understand at the front of the classroom. But everyone else did understand, so the natural conclusion I made was that they were smart and I was not. It took me several years to really catch up academically, since by the time I learned enough English to get what was going on, I had missed a lot of material that others had already learned. But it took even longer to change the habit of feeling dumber than everyone else. Even now, decades later, the ordinary insecurity or imposter syndrome that people (especially professors) feel can hit me in particularly sharp ways if I let my guard down. Maybe it's one of the reasons I gravitated toward philosophy, where nobody really knows what's going on. In fact, it may even be one of the reasons why I pursued academic studies at all—to prove, primarily to myself, that I wasn't that dumb kindergartener anymore. Who knows.

Remember that building good habits does not exclude addressing underlying emotional or psychological issues, though that's not exactly Aristotle's concern. This seems especially pertinent in the case of low self-esteem, whereas it seems somewhat less relevant in regards to being a cheap bastard. But in any case, the time comes when the bad habit needs to be replaced by a good habit, and this can only come about by acting as if you have the good habit, or at least not acting on, or actively resisting, the bad habit. Book VII is all about this, in fact, and because of that it's arguably the most important part of the *Ethics*. But in the meantime, enroll in that class, apply for that job, text that girl or boy, get to the gym, and even if it doesn't work out, at least you tried. And you deserve to try. And if you're a narcissist, stay quiet and learn that it's okay for the attention not to be on you sometimes, and that begging for attention is beneath you.

Patience

"The man who is angry at the right things and with the right people, and, further, as he ought, when he ought, and as long as he ought, is praised." (IV.5)

The first story I told in this book (I think; I don't feel like scrolling up) was about me getting mad at traffic, which isn't so much a story as a permanent aspect of my personality. Just like all our emotions, anger is there for a reason, but just like all of them, it can do damage if it takes over our lives. This is so obvious as not to need illustration, but if you want an example, just think what would happen to your life if you actually did the things you imagine doing to your boss.

Like many of the other virtues, patience is a mean that leans more to one side than another, in order to correct a tendency most people have in the opposite direction. The tendency most people have, according to Aristotle, is to overdo it when they get mad, rather than underdo it. So the effort for most of us should be to bite our tongue (not literally please) and wait until we're calm before we address the issue that caused the anger in the first place. We become less objective when we're angry, and it's wiser to let ourselves calm down before we make any decisions. This is why we say things we regret when we're in a fight, and it's also why apologies, and accepting apologies, are an important part of human life.

However, and this is a big however, Aristotle's discussion on anger leads to the only place he seems to address what we might call "repression" today, and it's an interesting thing to think about, even if Aristotle might not have gotten all the details right. His approach is from a social perspective, as it often is. People who explode with anger when they're annoyed but then calm down and move on are easier to live with than people who hold it in and sulk for hours, or days, or weeks. Worst of all are those who are always angry and never admit it, even to themselves—people we might call passive aggressive. Aristotle is unduly polite in describing them: "such people are most troublesome to themselves and to their dearest friends."

This is an interesting shift for Aristotle. On the one hand, the goal of this book is virtue, which is defined as a kind of excellence. On the other hand, when it comes to anger, Aristotle presents the second and third best options as well as the best. When he describes courage, for example, he works through many different possibilities in order to distinguish them from true courage so that we (or the soldier who is the carrier of true courage) know what we're really shooting for. Here, where he seems to be speaking to the average Joe, or maybe even the below-average-Joe-who-is-kind-of-a-jerk, he presents the non-virtuous alternatives almost as stepping stones. Maybe the soldier with true courage is less rare than the person who is angry "at the right things and with the right people, and, further, as he ought, when he ought, and as long as he ought." That doesn't make one better or worse than the other, it just shows the relative complexity of the social life within which true virtuous patience exists.

So the message seems to be that, while you're striving for perfect patience, err on the side of caution as always; that is, avoid acting on your anger. But don't do that in a way that will cause you to sulk like an annoying child, or become passive aggressive like an annoying adult. Losing your temper for a second and then apologizing immediately, even if it's not virtue, makes you easier to live with than the alternatives. Maybe an even better intermediate step would be to try to talk about your anger with honesty and as much calm as you can muster. But, as always, what do I know? The very angels weep hearing the things I say when I'm driving.

Politeness

> "For he seems to be concerned with the pleasures and pains of social life; and wherever it is not honorable, or is harmful, for him to contribute pleasure, he will refuse, and will choose rather to give pain." (IV. 6)

Next Aristotle discusses three virtues related to conversation: politeness, honesty, and wit. I'll spend a little time on each of them, but it's interesting to note that he wraps up his enumeration of the virtues with the ones having to do with talking (shame, the last section of this Book, isn't quite a virtue). For Aristotle, talking isn't just a thing that humans do; it's *the* thing that humans do—their defining characteristic. Remember earlier he defined the human being as the "rational animal," and distinguished the two senses of that as the life of society and the life of the intellect. But talking (the Greek word *logos*) is about both of those things ("rational" comes from the Latin word *ratio*, which corresponds to the Greek word *logos*). We can't be truly social without communication, and we can't be fully rational without words. Speaking is the activity that brings all of this together, and is somehow the thing we do that is most quintessentially human. So doing it well is important, and doing it badly is harmful.

The first talk-based virtue, which I'm calling "politeness," has to do with disagreeing in a civil way. It's one thing to be a total pushover and just go along with what anyone or everyone says; it's another thing to be so stubborn a contrarian that you deliberately disagree with something simply because people say it. The first type would be too chicken to have (or at least state) an opinion before checking their Twitter feed to make sure it was acceptable; the second type would nervously check the Billboard charts to make sure their favorite band never got too popular.

The virtue in this case would be to have your own thoughtful opinions and concerns and beliefs, and be able to disagree with someone in the right way, time, and place, and agree with someone similarly. If your friend is about to have their tenth tequila shot of the night, it's time for you to speak up, even if it hurts their drunken feelings (they won't remember tomorrow anyway). On the other hand, if someone you can't stand makes a valid point, it's the mark of decency to admit it. I usually hate making generalizations about "people today," but it's irritating to see the words "fascist" and "snowflake" thrown around in place of actual argumentation. Just because someone doesn't care about something you care about doesn't make them a fascist, and just because someone cares about something you don't care about doesn't make them a snowflake. Maybe having a conversation trying to utilize this virtue would do more good than name calling. On the other hand, sometimes people really are fascists or snowflakes, or, more often than not, both.

Honesty/Verbal Modesty

> "The man who observes the mean is one who calls a thing by its own name, being truthful both in life and in word, owning to what he has, and neither more nor less." (IV.7)

I happen to be really bad at accepting compliments. This is probably related to the fact that I hate almost any attention being placed on me, which is related to some insecurity or shyness or acne or God knows what else. Yes, I'm aware of the irony of this fact combined with literally any of my jobs or the fact that I write books like this. But at least I don't do podcasts.

I forgot where I was going with this. Oh yeah: being awkward or uncomfortable at accepting compliments is (I think) the less-harmful vice related to the virtue of honesty, or, as I subtitle it, verbal modesty. Bragging or wanting to be the center of attention all the time is the more harmful vice. I know people who literally break out into hives when they aren't the center of attention. Less extremely, there are many who feel some kind of emotional pain when they don't get the attention or credit they think they deserve. This can lead to anger or harm friendships, or it can turn into "humble bragging" or throat-clearing, all of which are bad for both the individual doing them and the people around him. It's also worth noting that the vice of bragging and that of excessive self-deprecation can even be contained in the same person, which is a rare thing for opposite vices. I'm proud to say I have mastered this combination.

The solution, that is, the virtue, is actually pretty simple: just speak truthfully about yourself when it's appropriate, and otherwise be attentive to the conversation. If someone compliments you, say thank you and move on—maybe even talk about them. You might discover at some point that not being the center of attention all the time isn't the end of the world, and that even when you are the center of attention, it doesn't last forever and isn't the essence of happiness.

A good friend of mine with about 900 graduate degrees was skilled at graciously bringing others into the conversation to take the attention away from himself. I noticed him many times asking others about things that I knew for a fact he knew, just to allow others to share the spotlight. And he did this so smoothly that hardly anyone could notice. But I noticed. You can't pull one over on me, pal.

This virtue is pretty obviously connected to magnanimity or self-esteem, but I think we might have a more direct ability to bring it about in ourselves. We might not have immediate access to our self-esteem, but we can certainly control what we say most of the time. At the very least, those of us who are attention whores can practice silent listening when others speak, without interjecting (I have students that would benefit from this, and I know this because I was myself a student who would have benefitted from this). And those of us who are compliment-repellent can blush and say thanks without making a joke about how lousy our sermon was, which is really just fishing for more compliments, . . . which is really dumb and I should stop doing it.

Wit

> "Those who joke in a tasteful way are called ready-witted, which
> implies a sort of readiness to turn this way and that; for such sallies are
> thought to be movements of the character." (IV.8)

The Name of the Rose recounts the fictional adventures of a monk who ends up discovering the long-lost second book of Aristotle's *Poetics*, which was about comedy. Unfortunately this discovery was never made in reality, and what Aristotle would have said about this topic can only be guessed at. This is one of the few places in his extant works where we get a glimpse at his thoughts, since according to him wit is one of the virtues.

The fact that it's a virtue, meaning a habit of doing something well, rather than a set of pre-written rules about what is or isn't offensive or a general injunction to "push the envelope," gives us a sophistication we should expect from Aristotle by now. Humor is a human thing, and just like all human things, it's about balance rather than extremity, and about the people you're with more than about abstract principles. Moreover, the fact that wit is a virtue mentioned in the *Ethics* at all means that humor is an important part of human life, not a trifle to be treated as if it doesn't matter. That's because resting and spending time with friends (what Aristotle' would call "amusement") is important. It (usually) doesn't make us money; it's the reason we make money at all. And so making your friends laugh is a good and virtuous act, and a central part of human life.

This is exactly why it's important to do this well rather than badly. While Aristotle might agree that we should remember it's "just a joke," he would also agree that some jokes are harmful. On the other hand, a lot of jokes need a victim. The victim could be you yourself, which is one of my favorite kinds of humor. It could be the person you're speaking to, which would require a high level of wit to pull off (because the idea is to make them laugh at themselves). It could be a foible of parents or children or siblings, or the human race in general.

However, just pointing out a flaw isn't a joke either. The way it's pointed out, the words used, the timing, the audience, the time and place the joke is made, are all factors. In fact, perhaps the most important factor is the person telling the joke, which is simply to say that the virtue of wit is possessed by the person, not the audience or the situation (though being able to take a joke is also part of this virtue).

The character or *ethos* of the person telling the joke is essential because it determines their intention. If your intention is to hurt someone, not make them laugh, you are not telling a joke. This is why people aren't being "over-sensitive" when they are offended if someone with a racist or anti-Catholic past makes a racist or anti-Catholic joke. This virtue, therefore, requires some real self reflection, both in understanding your own prejudices and your own intentions.

Even with the right character and intention, time and place, subject matter and everything else, the joke still has to be clever and surprising in one way or another. Whatever you think of cleverness, whether or not something is surprising is relative to your audience, and this is another place where skill, knowledge, and experience come into play in virtue. Beyond that, Aristotle notes in passing, things get hard to define.

The other, less skill-based, half of wit is the ability to take a joke, and this is just as important. In the same way that self-awareness is needed for the jokester to know his own intentions in telling the joke, it is needed for the audience member when he gets offended. Perhaps the joke really was offensive, but perhaps you have a stick up your butt. First remove the stick from your own butt, and then you will see clearly to remove the splinter from your brother's butt.

Shame

"Shame may be said to be conditionally a good thing." (IV.9)

Before shifting and spending an entire Book on the virtue of justice, Aristotle finishes his discussion on this group of moral virtues with a short chapter on shame, which he describes as a quasi-virtue. The reason it's not a virtue strictly speaking is that it has to do with bad actions, not good ones. In this way, it's similar to guilt, and I think there's a lot to be said about their other similarities. But I won't do that here.

Another reason why shame isn't really a virtue is because it's a feeling, and the other virtues are habits. However, I do think we can train our sense of shame in various ways, the way we can gain or lose habits, so I think the picture is a little more complicated. My first time playing mandolin at open mic I was embarrassed whenever I made a mistake, which was quite a bit. Though messing up a riff from an Irish song isn't an immoral act, the mess up does indicate a lack in the virtue of mandolin-playing, which is precisely what I was showcasing that night. But after what can loosely be called my performance, I returned to my seat and realized that nobody had pelted me with tomatoes or walked out indignantly because of my mistakes. So the next time I performed I was less embarrassed about messing up. Now, many performances later, I'm practically a pro. I mess up with comfort and ease.

The stupid example above illustrates how our sense of shame can be adjusted, and how losing some shame with certain things can sometimes be beneficial. I would never have performed at all if my embarrassment was all-powerful, and I know many people who are much better musicians than I am who have never worked up the courage to play in front of an audience. This is not to say that shamelessness is a virtue, only that shame can and should be moderated according to reason like any other habit. This would also apply when we despair or want to completely give up over a small mistake, or wake up in the middle of the night in a cold sweat because we remember and relive the intense humiliation we felt after throwing up in Ms. Martin's class in fourth grade. Sometimes shame needs to calm the hell down.

But it should not be destroyed—not because it's good or a virtue itself, but because of the kind of people we are and the kind of world we live in. Being virtuous because our mind knows it is best isn't always the most powerful motivation, and when that approach fails, a healthy sense of shame can be there as a safety net to stop us from messing up our lives and those of others. Maybe our reason alone can't stop us from giving in to some temptations, but a fear of getting caught can. This isn't ideal, of course, but this book isn't written for perfect saints, since they don't need it anyway. At the very least, it can be a step in the right direction—that is, a step toward real virtue. There will be a lot more about this in Book VII.

Passion Governed	More Likely Extreme	Virtue/Mean	Less Likely Extreme
Fear	Cowardice	Courage	Foolhardiness
Bodily desire	Intemperance	Temperance	Cold fishiness
Desire for money	Cheap bastardness	Generosity	Spendthriftiness
Self-esteem	Pusillanimity	Magnanimity	Narcissism
Anger	Jerkiness	Patience	Doormat

Examples of virtues and vices

Justice

In This Chapter:

Fairness, sharing, laws, inner conflict.

I think there's a problem that requires solving at this point in the book. Now that you, as the person reading Aristotle's advice and putting it into practice, have put your desires in check and trained them to obey reason (as if it's that easy), what is it exactly that is driving you now? Before, when we were vicious or incontinent people, we'd get up in the morning in order to pursue money or sex or honor in disordered ways. Now that those desires have been moderated, why are we waking up? I think Book V is the beginning of the answer to this question, though the complete answer isn't found until Book X (though it was hinted at in Book I). For now, though, we can work toward one answer: we get up in the morning because it is just.

Disambiguation

"Now 'justice' and 'injustice' seem to be ambiguous." (V.1)

One of Aristotle's favorite things to do was define words and distinguish different senses of them. Justice is a word that he must have gotten sick of defining while a student at Plato's Academy. The *Republic* of Plato spends a few hundred pages both defining and fleshing out what justice is and means, and by the end of it, you might not be any closer to the answer if you weren't paying really close attention. I'll probably refer to the *Republic* a bunch of times in the following pages, mostly because I like it a lot more than I like *Nicomachean Ethics* book V.

In any case, let's disambiguate. I'll organize this a little differently than Aristotle does, but I think it's basically the same idea. Justice can mean one of three things: it can be a word describing all moral virtue (like in the Bible when a guy is called "a just man"); it can mean the distinct virtue related to interacting with other people in regards to material goods; and it can mean legal justice, as in obeying civil laws. Most of *Ethics* V is about the second, the special virtue of justice, though it touches on all three senses.

There is a question that comes up here that is also at the heart of the *Republic*, which is whether there really is natural justice at all, or only legal justice. In other words, is there a real right and wrong that applies to everyone, everywhere, or are there only laws and customs that people need to obey just to avoid punishment or ostracization?

There's plenty to say about this question, and I've already said some in earlier chapters, but one way to argue for natural justice is to think about tyranny. If there were only legal justice, that is, if obeying the written civil laws was the only standard of right and wrong, on what grounds would it be legitimate to overthrow even the most brutal tyrant? If there was ever a reason for any revolution, it was because there must be some law above and beyond the written civil law. Otherwise we'd just be replacing one tyranny with another.

This "above and beyond" law is what people now call natural law, and I'll assume that it exists, and point out that basically everything in this book so far is nothing more than an expression of it. Natural law isn't so much a set of rules of what to do and not do as an understanding of human nature and the way it finds fulfillment and happiness, as opposed to misery and self-destruction.

So that's the distinction between civil and natural justice. The other distinction, between justice meaning "virtue in general" and justice as a special virtue, is more relevant to this chapter. Justice the special virtue has to do with "grasping," that is, with material goods and activities that have to do with other people. It's defined loosely as "the good of another." So let's start this chapter by thinking about others.

Common Good

> "Now the laws in their enactments on all subjects aim at the common advantage either of all or of the best or of those who hold power." (V.1)

Even though Aristotle distinguishes civil laws from natural justice, he does believe that there should be a deep connection between the two. As I'll discuss in a later section, the laws of the city, state, or country, aren't just about protecting each individual's rights to life, liberty, and property (a much later concept of laws found in John Locke). On the contrary, Aristotle sees civil laws as written and enforceable applications of natural justice that have to do with the community. So written laws, to really be laws and not pretenders, have to teach citizens the virtues that have to do with living together.

The fundamental principle that governs justice in every form is that the good of everyone (called the "common good") is more important than the good of anyone (that is, any individual). A related principle that is just as important is that the common good and each person's individual good are co-dependent. That is, what's good for me is ultimately the same as what's good for everyone, since my own happiness in various ways relies on the happiness of the people who are part of my community. If everyone around me is sad or destitute or angry at me, it will be a lot harder for me to be happy.

This is an important reversal of one of the versions of justice discussed early in Plato's *Republic* by a character named Thrasymachus. His version of justice is that anyone who can get away with it should do whatever they want. This implies that what's good for me is different from what's good for the people around me. Aristotle's starting point is the opposite. He sees the connection between each person's good and that of their city. While some thinkers would start from the idea that living in a society is basically a restriction of each person's freedom (even if this restriction is ultimately beneficial), and while Freud describes civilization as something that creates "discontent," Aristotle begins with the premise that living with others is the best way for anyone to live, and the only way to be happy.

The "just regime," or a good government, therefore writes laws to teach its citizens to live as though their own happiness is tied up with the good of all their neighbors—that is, it rewards justice towards others and it punishes injustice and selfishness. Any written law that is a real law supports this principle, and anything that doesn't isn't really a law, but an imposition of injustice by a tyrant.

These general principles are fairly clear, but of course their practical application is (like everything in politics) extremely difficult and requires its own set of skills and virtues. Aristotle will get to these eventually (in his next book, called the *Politics*), but he needs to first lay their foundation in the *Ethics*.

Relatives

> "This form of justice, then, is complete virtue, although not without qualification, but in relation to another." (V.1)

I've talked a bit about virtues being relative, that is, determined according to particular situations, though based on a human nature we all share in common. The right amount to eat for The Rock is different from the right amount for that little fellow who played Harry Potter. But the virtues are relative in another sense as well, in that each of them is related to some particular passion: courage is related to fear; temperance is related to sexual desire; magnanimity to one's desire for honor; liberality to the desire for wealth. They moderate and regulate desires and actions (the way these two connect is one topic of Book VII). But justice, in the sense of the particular virtue, isn't relative to any *passion*, but to *other people*.

This makes it, more than the virtues that we've seen in previous chapters, "objective," in that it is aimed at and determined by something outside the subject acting. It is, essentially, fairness. The child who wants to keep the toy that isn't hers learns a lesson about fairness: she has her own toys at home, and she wouldn't like it if someone took them. This is a step toward seeing others and their needs as equally important as hers, and that's what the virtue of justice is about. Its opposite, injustice, is like the selfishness of the child who wants all the toys to herself. There's something right about saying that justice is "all of virtue" and that injustice is "all of vice" as they relate to other people. Selfishness, as a character trait, is unwillingness to pay any attention to others or their needs, or to fairness itself.

Because there is something particularly "external" about justice, it relates in a special way to material goods, since they can be divided and diminished. If all of you are hungry and I eat the whole pizza, you stay hungry. But if I feel happy, my feeling of happiness doesn't detract from yours. If I read a book, there's nothing stopping you from reading it as well—even the same copy, when I'm not reading it. If I learn Sumerian, nobody loses anything by my gain. So activities like these aren't the ones that justice has to limit or regulate, only things that can be diminished by being shared. Justice is the virtue of pizza.

In the first couple books of the *Republic,* the characters offer various versions of a definition of justice. I won't go into who gives what definition and why (even though that's really interesting and important), but they range from "paying back what's owed" to "the advantage of the stronger" to "minding your business." These three definitions, though they are debated in the *Republic,* aren't necessarily contradictory. The connection between the three, and the aspect of justice that becomes the most important, both in the *Republic* and in Aristotle's works, is the community. Paying back what's owed: whether we realize it or not, our community has given us a lot, and because it's given us something, we owe it in various ways. The advantage of the stronger: the community is also stronger than any of us as an individual, and what's good for it is more important than what's good for any one of us. Minding your business: our work and focus is ultimately defined by the needs of the community around us. Putting the needs of others, in the sense of the community, before our own is the heart of what justice is about, and putting ourselves before our whole community is the essence of injustice. The trick in all this is to see how what's good for my community is one and the same as what's good for me, and that selfishness is ultimately self-destruction.

Legislating Morality

> "The things that tend to produce virtue taken as a whole are those of
> the acts prescribed by the law which have been prescribed with a view
> to the common good." (V.2)

One of the interwoven threads of Plato's *Republic* is the topic of tyranny and the tyrant, which comes to a culmination in Book IX. There Socrates argues a point introduced much earlier in the dialogue: that the tyrant, of all people, is the most miserable. This stands contrary to what the Average Joe or Typical Thrasymachus would guess. You'd think the tyrant, the guy who gets whatever he wants without any consequences, would be the happiest—what is happiness, in fact, other than getting what you want? And yet the exact opposite is true: the tyrant, who gets whatever he wants without consequence, is beyond unhappy, and not because of any future punishment or betrayal or uprising against him. He's miserable already, and more miserable than any of the people he oppresses.

I think there's an instinctual truth to this that many people might recognize, and I don't want to go over the arguments for it in the *Republic*. In fact, I think you could argue (and I bet someone has) that the *Nicomachean Ethics* and the *Politics* together (not only the *Politics*) are Aristotle's own version of, or reply to, the *Republic*. That is to say, by the end of Aristotle's book, and by extension and to a much lesser degree by the end of this book, you'll have your own answer to why the tyrant is the unhappiest of human beings. But let's take it for granted here, and I'll sneak away with a hint that the answer is in the material I'll discuss in Book VII. Yes, I like suspense.

If it's (assumed to be) the case that whoever gets everything they want without consequence is miserable, and if it's (definitely) the case that people getting everything they want (including other people's stuff) are bad for the city, then laws restraining selfishness are good both for the city and for each citizen. Stealing is bad for the victim and for neighborhood morale. But stealing is also bad for the thief. So when stealing is made illegal, that prohibition is good for *everyone*, even if thieves take it personally. Even if they truly believe it best for them to take what belongs to others, it isn't.

This leads to one of the most pivotal differences between Aristotle's understanding of civil laws and that of John Locke, who was admired by the founders of the American republic. For Locke, the laws of the state were meant to protect each citizen's "life, liberty, and property." For Aristotle, the laws of the state were meant to teach each citizen how to live a good and virtuous life; laws aren't only there to protect cities from tyrants—they are there to protect tyrants from themselves. The reason why there are civil laws, according to Aristotle, is that it is the job of the government to legislate morality. Not exactly an American libertarian cup of tea, but there it is.

I used the word "teach" when talking about how the laws operate, and I think that's exactly Aristotle's intention. The most important role of the government, for him, is the education of citizens, and education here doesn't mean learning multiplication tables and training for the cubicle workforce. Education itself fundamentally means growing in moral virtue. The laws are to be written to teach the citizens good habits, to encourage them to be morally good, caring toward what is right for themselves and their fellow citizens, and discourage them from being tyrannical to themselves and their fellow citizens.

This introduces a very interesting and very difficult question: what if you happen to live in a country that has a different conception of laws than Aristotle had? What if, somewhere in the foundation of your state, John Locke had more of a say than Aristotle (which, by the way, I'm not sure was entirely the case in America)? Even worse, let's say we're convinced that Aristotle's view was the right one. Should we, as citizens of such a city, make an effort to change its constitution to be more like one Aristotle envisioned, or should we respect it as is and do our best to live as good citizens within its boundaries? I repeat that this is a very difficult question, and even within Aristotle's writings there are heavy warnings about the danger of regime change. Which is why I don't have an answer for you at all. Figure it out yourself.

Distributive, Rectificatory, Reciprocal Justice

Ok, so we're still assuming that living tyrannically isn't the right way to live, and taking what doesn't belong to you is bad both for your community and for you. But similarly, letting someone else take advantage of you unjustly is also bad for your community, and for them, and if you care about your neighbor, the last thing you'd want him to become is a thief. So what gets to decide what's fair if not your desires or those of your neighbor?

Somewhere in the *Politics* Aristotle defines law as "intellect without passion." That's simply to say that what the law prescribes as just and fair should be impartial and unemotional. Fair is fair, and fairness is something defined by reason, not by anger or selfishness. And sometimes the best way to keep passion out of it when it comes to material goods, is to just let math do the work instead. So this little section is about the different mathematical ways Aristotle discusses the just sharing and interchange of material goods. There are three types of justice he names that are related to this: distributive, rectificatory, and reciprocal.

Distributive justice is about, well, distribution. Let's say each of the five original members of Guns N' Roses spends an equal amount of time on stage and puts in an equal amount of work otherwise. Taken alone, that would imply that they should get an equal amount of pay when the checks and cocaine come rolling in. However, let's say that Axl and Slash each put in twice as much effort as the other members. That would mean that they should each get twice the amount the others get, so the proportion of distribution would be set accordingly. This becomes most obvious in large corporations, where the CEO obviously works 100,000,000 times harder than anyone else and deserves that many times more money. Side note: Aristotle calls this "geometric" proportion, I guess because he's imagining a rectangle growing and shrinking, but whose sides stay the same ratio in relation to each other.

Rectificatory justice is about the restoration of something taken. So let's say there's one pound of cocaine that all four original members of Black Sabbath have to split. That means four ounces for each of them. But let's say Ozzy snorts an extra ounce, leaving only three ounces for Geezer Butler. This grave injustice cries out to heaven for rectification. Accordingly, the next day, Ozzy lets Geezer have an extra ounce from his pile. Justice has been done. Aristotle calls this "arithmetic" proportion, since it has to do with two sides of an equal sign: 4 ounces of cocaine + 1 ounce of cocaine = 6 ounces of cocaine—1 ounce of cocaine, or, more abstractly, $4+1=6-1$. Apologies if cocaine is measured using the metric system instead of the System of Her Majesty.

Reciprocal justice has to do with marketplace values and transactions, and is what I'd imagine someone would read about in a textbook on economics if there is such a thing. It's here that the work put into an item for sale, its rarity, the need for it, the value of the currency in question, all come into play, and Aristotle goes into it in more detail than I am, but still not much more.

A last type of justice Aristotle mentions is equity, which is a distribution of goods based not entirely on abstract mathematical principles, but rather on particular circumstances and relative need. I don't think I'd be going out on any limb saying that if a billionaire was living lavishly and on his porch there was a poor man dying of hunger, it would be justice for the poor man to get some of the rich man's food even if he didn't necessarily work to earn it. Aristotle calls equity "better than justice" because it "corrects" the abstract universal principle to the actual particular.

Now go figure out what counts as a porch.

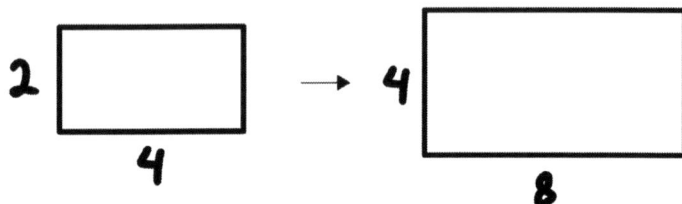

Figure 7: Types of justice

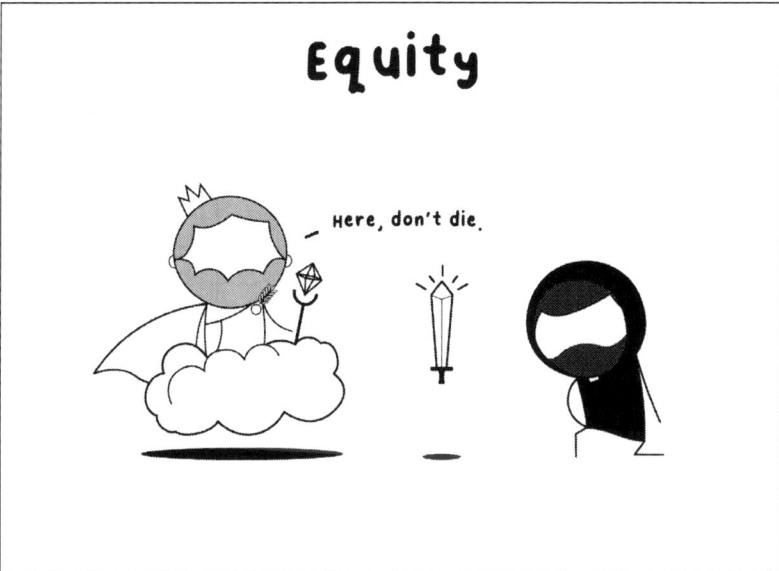

Figure 7: Types of justice (*cont.*)

Rulers and Communities

> "This is why we do not allow a *man* to rule, but *rational principle*, because a man behaves thus in his own interests and becomes a tyrant." (V.6)

If justice is the virtue regulating our behavior toward others, and others generally means others in a community, then community leadership must require the supreme kind of justice in the ruler. In a sense, the ruler, whoever he or she or they is, have to be superhuman, because plain old humans have trouble not putting themselves first, or letting their own wants cloud their minds or skew their decisions. I don't like to be judgmental, but I'd guess that might be why so many senators end up so rich so quickly.

Unfortunately, and I mean that with all my heart, superhumans aren't real. What we're left with are several billion selfish meatbags who can't even walk through walls, much less shoot lasers out of their eyes or act with perfect justice. What's to be done about the community then? How can we find rulers when nobody is worthy of rulership? Do we just accept the fact of tyranny and retreat into cynicism? Or worse, do we blind ourselves into believing one particular meatbag really does have our best interests in mind, or worst of all, an entire political party?

The upbringing and education of real leaders is a topic that both Plato and Aristotle spent a lot of time thinking and writing about, and it requires someone smarter and more specialized than I am to write about what they wrote about, but the importance of the topic needs to be understood. Thinking naively that leaders will raise themselves, or pop out of the ground, or snap into virtue when elected, is exactly the kind of thinking that causes the ruin of civilizations and the corruption of religious institutions. And thinking that leadership is itself a virtue that is independent of all the other virtues, that someone can be a good leader without first being a good person, is Machiavelli much more than it's Aristotle, and I'll let you grapple with who might be right about that.

On the other hand, and speaking of Machiavelli, to turn to cynicism and believe that virtue and leadership can't be taught at all, that we're stuck with selfish meatbags and nothing more, is just to invite and accept tyranny as a matter of fact. If the virtues can't be taught, then forget education, and if political leadership can't be taught, then forget democracy. I don't think I could educate a political leader very well if I tried, but one thing I think is an absolute prerequisite is that they really truly care about the community they are supposed to serve, not just pretend to. I don't think I'm alone when I say that I find it hard to believe in the sincerity of many politicians. Because this book is deliberately not about religion, I won't make any comment about bishops.

In the meantime, while we're making a mess trying to figure out how to raise up both leaders and decent citizens, Aristotle has a quicker solution. Instead of letting any individual person rule, let there be a rule of law. If there are decent laws in place, simply obeying and enforcing them can be completely dispassionate, which means that the personal imperfection of the people in charge becomes less of a problem. This is why it's infuriating when we see the law applied to some people and not to others—for example, when a rapist avoids going to prison because of the wealth of his father. Because this book is deliberately not about religion, I won't make any comment about priests.

Natural Justice

"With us there is something that is just even by nature, yet all of it is changeable; but still some is by nature, some not by nature." (V.7)

Let's say more about natural justice—or, more precisely, let me say more explicitly what I think is already implicit in what's been said, since I think both Plato and Aristotle give us their answers as to what natural justice really is by writing entire books about it—the *Republic* and the *Nicomachean Ethics*, respectively. But again, let's assume the opposite of our view is true to see where it leads. If there is no natural justice, and all justice is by convention, or what we'd call "culturally conditioned," that would mean what we're used to hearing, that morality itself is relative—not to human beings or particular conditions, but relative in the sense of not real, only an illusion of the culture around us. There really isn't a right or wrong, just or unjust, good and evil, but only what our culture, or we as individuals, determine to be so.

Remember that this claim about relativity is absolute. It's different than saying that the moral norms of any given culture are imperfect. Maybe your grandfather's attitude toward interracial marriage was wrong, but maybe his thoughts about smoking were right. That assumes that there is a correct answer to the right, or at least best, way for people to live. And even if it's not precise (as we saw in Book I), it's still real.

But this isn't about correcting flaws in cultural judgments about right and wrong. If there isn't natural justice at all, it means there is no right and wrong, and no correcting things. If you believe that sex before marriage is okay but that adultery is wrong, you're not a moral relativist. You just disagree with the content of morality. If you were a moral relativist, you'd believe that both of them are neither right nor wrong, along with slavery, murder, chemical warfare, rape, and everything else.

We might disagree about whether some activity is right or wrong, or about why it's right or wrong, or about what it is that makes something right or wrong, but I don't think I've met anyone who really doesn't believe in right and wrong at all. When we're robbed, we're emotionally upset, but I don't think that's an irrational emotion. I think we're angry because an objective injustice has been committed, and we are the victims. A moral relativist would, it seems to me, have to say that feeling upset when you're robbed (or the victim of any crime) is just a feeling, and not based on any reason or reality. I suppose it's a weakness in my brain that I have difficulty imagining anyone really believing that. It's certainly funny to notice many of the same people claiming to believe in moral relativism championing (or, for that matter, forcing) democracy, or feminism, or contraception, on cultures that don't like them. It's difficult to see why we should do anything like that if all morality is culturally conditioned. Unless you mean that everyone else's morality is culturally conditioned and yours isn't, in which case you're very much an inheritor of the attitude of the British Empire.

A better analysis might be to say that all moral "norms" are culturally conditioned in the sense that they are different, imperfect, expressions of a real underlying natural justice. That natural justice is, according to Aristotle, not a very precise thing in itself due to the infinitely particular circumstances of human life, but it is real nonetheless. If that's the case, it's possible for cultures to not only change but improve, and for them, and us, to be critiqued. It's not so much that polygamy and monogamy are equal in that they're neither right nor wrong, but that sex is a weird thing and it's better to have some rules about it than none at all. If we can have that as a starting point, we might be able to understand each other better. But if one culture, namely the super-postmodern West, decrees that all rules about sex are silly outdated cultural prisons, and imposes that view on the rest of the world (and backwards into the rest of ignorant history), that is not moral relativism but moral imperialism. And if you're going to be a moral imperialist, at least admit that you're not a relativist.

Divided Souls

"The incontinent man voluntarily harms himself." (V.9)

Last week I borrowed a video game system from a friend to see if I wanted to buy one for myself. The game, which will go unnamed but rhymes with *The Zegend of Lelda: Weath of the Brild*, was exquisite and, like all beautiful things, dangerous. In an act of great virtue, I made a rule for myself not to play it before 10 PM, and only if I'd gotten my work done for that day, and I obeyed that rule. The problem was that once I started playing, the game created ruptures in the passage of time. I would look up at the clock at 10:15. Five minutes later I'd look again, and it would be 1:30 AM. Another five minutes and it would be 3:30, and I hadn't gotten up to drink water or use the bathroom for over five hours.

The first day that happened I gave myself a mulligan. After all, I hadn't played a video game like that for over a decade and didn't remember the effect they had on general relativity. On day 2 I braced myself, and decided to try harder to be responsible with the device capable of such destruction. But despite my best efforts, the same thing happened. Day 3 came, but by then I was hooked. I knew perfectly well that the game would suck me in, and that if I looked up at midnight and kept playing, I'd be up till past 3 again. But despite my knowledge, I did it anyway. The next day, I gave the game back to my friend. I'm apparently not responsible enough to have it.

This is a stupid example of how things like addictions work, but it's a pattern that applies to a lot of things in life, from games to fast food to relationships. Despite our knowledge that doing something will hurt us, we still do it. Aristotle re-introduces this dynamic at the end of Book V, because there is a kind of analogy with injustice in it: because there are different aspects of our psyche, it is possible for one part to hurt another unjustly. My desire for fun ended up hurting my sleep schedule (and making me feel tired or have a headache the whole next day). Analyzed differently, there was a conflict between what my passions desired and what my reason knew was best. This relationship between reason and the passions is a very central topic that we've already run into, but it won't get full treatment till Book VII. Before we're ready to learn about the proper relationship between reason and the passions, we need to understand the proper workings of reason.

Book VI

Intellectual Virtues

In This Chapter:

Thinkin', makin', doin', rulin', more thinkin'.

Who Cares

> "Hence it is necessary with regard to the states of the soul also, not
> only that this true statement should be made, but also that it should be
> determined what correct reason is and what is the standard that fixes it."
> (VI.1)

Let's say you're dying of a horrible disease and you went to the doctor. You
ask her in desperation which medicine you should take, and she answers,
with total accuracy, "that which would cure you." Later, you die.

This whole book we've been hearing about how our actions and desires should be "in accord with reason." Isn't that just another way of saying
that they should be "what they should be"? Are we just going in circles, or
is there some real answer to all this? Well, go back to the doctor above. Just
because she gave you a pedantic answer doesn't mean it's a bad answer.
She's technically correct, but her answer just implies another question you

should ask: What is the medicine that will cure me? The answer to that is something that a doctor would know. Similarly, "what should my actions and desires be?" is something that ethics can teach you.

But there's more to the story of what's "in accord with reason." In order to figure that out, Aristotle spends this sixth Book of the *Ethics* discussing the different virtues of reason—what are labeled the "intellectual virtues." His own excuse for doing this is a little more complicated: not only should we study the virtues of the mind because they'll show us what we should really do, morally speaking, but also because these virtues are worth studying for their own sake.

He's got a point: if we've spent so much time talking about what the right habits are when it comes to feeling and acting, why would we neglect what is arguably the most important thing that we do, which is thinking? If the arguments of Book I are right, these virtues might be the most important ones for us to understand. On the other hand, not every definition he makes here is directly applicable to living a happy life. As usual, I will spend more time on everyday things and less time on scholarly debates, even though those can (occasionally) be interesting.

The first thing he does here is repeat a distinction he made earlier in the *Ethics* between the "parts of the soul" that are *rational* and *non-rational*. The rational, remember, refers to the mind and the non-rational to other processes like breathing and digestion; in between there are the feelings, which are *semi-rational* because they can both affect the mind and be affected by it. The next distinction is within the rational part of the soul, and that's between *science* and *deliberation*. The mind is able to think about things that are unchanging and invariable: the fact that triangles have three sides or electrons have a negative charge. This ability is called "scientific reason" (it's somewhat broader than what we'd call science today, but that's not very important here). On the other hand, the mind can also think about things that are changeable and variable: whether I'm sleepy or hungry, whether it's raining outside, whether the economy is doing well. These variable things are important to think about when we make everyday decisions, so the ability to understand them is called "deliberative reason."

There's a lot more that I'll say about both science and deliberation below, but the basic distinction is between discovery and decision. We *discover* science and *decide* on our deliberations. We don't decide what would be the best sum of 2 and 2, we discover it. We don't discover whether we will go swimming or jogging, we decide it.

Choice

> "Since moral virtue is a state of character concerned with choice, and choice is deliberate desire, therefore both the reasoning must be true and the desire right, if the choice is to be good, and the latter must pursue just what the former asserts." (VI.2)

What exactly is a decision or a choice? Aristotle doesn't quite settle on one definition, but offers two: he says it's either "reasoned desire" or "desiring reason." That is, choice is some unified act of the two parts of the soul we're calling reason and the passions. While it's possible that Aristotle gave two definitions because he wasn't quite sure which one was right, I also think it's possible that Aristotle thinks there are two forms of choosing. One form, "reasoned desire," is where reason takes the lead, perceives something as good, and brings desire along in one way or another. For example, you could wake up in the morning, think about how going for a jog would be a great way to start your day, and then enjoy your jog. The other form, "desiring reason," is where desire takes the lead and drags reason along with it, like when you don't feel like going for a jog, and convince yourself that jogging is for losers anyway.

In either case, these two parts of the soul have to come to some sort of agreement, even if one or the other is reluctant. You could go for the jog not happily but bitterly, but you still went for the jog. The choice was made by reason, and even if your desire hasn't quite been "reasoned" yet, your decision was. If there's total conflict between what you think you should do and what you want to do, and there's a stalemate about which of the two is stronger, there's no choice at all. In the example of jogging, however, the result is the same as the second option of "desiring reason:" not choosing to jog is the same as choosing not to jog.

There's another problem built into this definition, one that isn't really resolved until the next Book. For a choice to be good, Aristotle says, two conditions are required: "the reasoning must be true and the desire right." So for a perfectly good choice, going for a jog really does need to be the right thing to do, and you really do need to want it. That means that the bitter jog, where you're going against your desires but jogging anyway, isn't quite good—or quite good yet. It's better than not jogging at all, but because you're doing it partially against your own desires (we say "against your will," but that's not quite precise), it won't be that great of a jog. How you go from jogging bitterly to jogging happily is, again, the topic of Book VII.

Book VI is about the first requirement, making sure that reasoning is true. While he gets fairly technical in describing this, the basic idea is that *reasoning is true when it follows reality*: whether or not it is *really* a good thing for you to go for that jog is something that can be figured out by reasoning well. If your knees are bad, or if your blood sugar is low, or if you're likely to be robbed and murdered, these realities might change the result of true reasoning, and maybe it's best to stay home and do some push ups instead.

Science, Intuition, and Wisdom

> "The object of scientific knowledge is of necessity. Therefore it is eternal; for things that are of necessity in the unqualified sense are all eternal." (VI.3)

So how do we know whether reasoning is true? In one way, answering this is the goal of all of philosophy, or at least a branch of it we now call epistemology. But Aristotle knows very well that ethics would be a dead end, and society would completely collapse, if everyone needed to understand the *Posterior Analytics* before they could make good choices and lead good lives. So he gives a basic, practical outline of some of the core concepts here.

In this section I'll summarize three of them: science (*episteme* in Greek), intuition (*nous*), and wisdom (*sophia*). Note that these words and concepts are debated by philosophers and scholars, so what follows is just one possible interpretation of how they relate to each other in the thought of Aristotle. They also relate to other mental activities that I discuss in more detail in later sections.

Science, in Aristotle's definition, is *demonstrated reasoning of necessary things*. "Demonstrated" means that the more something is based on guesswork or probability, rather than strict logical reasoning, the less it's a science. "Necessary things" means whatever cannot be other than it is, so the more variable the object, the less strict is the science that deals with it. For both these reasons, logic and mathematics are almost universally posited as the most sciency of sciences, and other sciences placed in a kind of spectrum beneath them based on how close they are to them in demonstration and necessity. Note that, in Aristotle's usage, this isn't a black-and-white distinction: there can be studies that are "more" or "less" scientific. Just because something isn't as demonstrative or necessary as mathematics doesn't mean it's just opinion—so even ethics, as complicated and bound up with material conditions as it is, is still a science, even if not the most precise because its objects are so changeable.

Intuition is the word I'm using to translate *nous*, which here indicates *our grasp of ultimate principles*. What it means for a principle to be "ultimate" means that it sits on the edge of knowledge, and isn't provable or justified by anything before it; it simply has to be accepted. There are two "edges" of knowledge that Aristotle describes: one is sensible knowledge; the other is knowledge of the most abstract principles. Science (the topic of the last paragraph) is built on the foundation of both these edges, but it doesn't and can't prove them.

For example, we can assert some statement like "all humans have skin." A scientist would ask why we assert that—what are the reasons we use to demonstrate the truth of that statement—and we could answer in various ways. In the end, though, a statement like that has to be based on some sort of observation, or set of observations, like "every human anyone has ever seen has skin," or "Fred over here has skin." This kind of reasoning is called "induction," and carries with it some immense philosophical problems that I won't go into here, but the point is that it is based on one of the "edges" of knowledge, which is sense observation. We accept that our senses give us some access to reality, and this acceptance is done by *nous* or intuition—it isn't something that itself is proven by science. It's a different kind of activity that our mind does.

The other "edge" is the apprehension of the most abstract principles. We can demonstrate "downward" from the definition of a straight line on a Euclidean plane, and write a proof that all triangles, by definition, have angles that add up to a straight line. This, for the record, is called a process of "deduction." But we can't write a proof that straight lines are straight—that's just an idea we accept and build on. That's probably why Euclid didn't even try to prove it—it's his fourth *definition*, but not a proposition or proof. Again, Aristotle has a special word for the apprehension and acceptance of these abstract principles, which is *nous* or intuition. It's fascinating to me that scientific knowledge, for Aristotle, has not one but two "edges" or foundations—the senses as well as abstract concepts. It's also interesting that the most foundational foundation is the senses, not the abstract concepts, since

Aristotle believes that we learn even the most abstract principles through the senses. Later philosophy of science might have a lot to learn from him. But that's a topic for another book.

Finally, wisdom or *sophia*, at least here, is a combination of both *episteme* (science) and *nous* (intuition). The wise person is the one who has *both* the correct apprehension of ultimate principles *as well as* the ability to make necessary deductions from them. Here's one example to show that this really is relevant to ethics, not just to more abstract sciences. A wise person would observe many people doing a certain activity—let's say sitting alone in the dark eating chips and playing video games for weeks at a time. It would also be observed that those doing this activity end up physically and emotionally unhealthy. These observations, based on the senses, would be apprehended and accepted by intuition. A simple induction would conclude that this activity is one that is unhealthy for human beings, and a simple deduction would say that if you are human, you should get outside and eat something besides chips once in a while. We might not always (or ever) do this process of reasoning in any explicit way, but it is something we do implicitly all the time.

Art

"All art is concerned with coming into being." (VI.4)

Science is about discovering unchanging things. Art, in contrast, is about changing things—both in the sense of changing *things*, as well as in the sense of *changing* things. Aristotle doesn't mean only artsy-fartsy things like paintings and poems and songs when he says *techne*, but any kind of production or making. Because we haven't yet developed the technology to create out of nothing, everything we make is, in one way or another, a rearrangement or combination of things that are already around. I think this even applies to ideas or imaginative things we come up with. Lamassu are imaginative creations combining "head of a bearded man," "eagle wings," and "bull torso," which are all individually things that we learned about in the boring old regular world. The same thing happens when we take dead trees and turn them into furniture, or move air waves around to make words, or cut compressed carbon mined by now-dead slaves and turn it into a symbol of everlasting love until the divorce.

Like science, art is a virtue that requires practice to perfect, as any artist knows. Like all the virtues, it's possible for some people to have more potential for art, or for certain types of art, even before they begin to develop it. But again like all the virtues, it doesn't get perfected unless it's practiced. If it's ignored, even the greatest talent is like a sleeping giant.

As a distinct virtue, art has a lot to do with the medium through which it's expressed. Woodworkers need good hands and knowledge of wood. Musicians need a good ear and a soul attuned to tunes. Poets need facility with words. Because art is about making, and making always uses something preexisting, that preexisting thing has to be something the artist knows, knows how to manipulate, and in some way cares about. Remember also that virtues have to do with pleasure and pain, so the real artist isn't just someone who can make a thing, but someone who can make a thing with pleasure. This is why it's pleasant even to observe a real artist at work—because their skill and the pleasure they take in their work becomes apparent to those watching. I've recently discovered videos online showing professional cobblers repair shoes, and I'm not embarrassed to say that watching them is fascinating.

An interesting note that I've mentioned before is about how the production of art and the intention of the artist often work in opposite directions. The first thing the novelist conceives, the novel itself, is the last thing that actually comes into being. But in order to have the novel, the novelist needs an old-timey typewriter and some paper, which means she needs to go into her office overlooking the lake, which means she needs to walk there from the bedroom, which means she needs to get up out of bed. The last thing she thinks about, getting out of bed, is the first thing that she does. Actual novelists (I remember reading Poe say this somewhere) often describe writing their stories very literally backwards—they think of how they want it to end and they figure out how the story gets there. Even if this isn't always the exact case with every single novelist or artist, I bet some version of this happens much of the time.

On the other hand, not everybody is an artist, and I should get back to the point. One big reason Aristotle talks about art in the *Ethics* at all is to show that it's *not* directly related to happiness—not for everyone. If it were, it would mean that non-artists aren't capable of being happy. On the contrary, happiness is something related to a human nature we all share, according to Aristotle. But more to the point, happiness isn't art because it's not production and doesn't require a material medium. Happiness is not something we *make* but something we *do*. It's not a production or a product, it's an activity.

Practical Wisdom

"With the presence of one quality, practical wisdom, will be given all the virtues." (VI.13)

If it hasn't become clear already, I sometimes tend to be an irascible person—that is, I'm kind of a jerk. Knowing this about myself is hopefully a step toward a cure, but it's not an instantaneous fix. The jerkiness in me is something that can survive scrutiny, and simply being aware of it does not cause its immediate destruction. Thus I am occasionally in a situation where I'll be around someone whom I find annoying for no rational reason (it could really be anyone), and know that my irritation is unreasonable, yet still feel it. Even worse, it is difficult, if not impossible, to know how my internal irritation affects my outward actions. Perhaps my tone of voice, or the words I choose to use, or the things I notice about them, are different than they would have been without my irritation. Not only are these things difficult to control, in the moment they are difficult even to judge.

I'll talk in the next Book about how to eventually change habits like this, and offer Aristotle's analysis of this dynamic, but there is a meantime solution that is not only useful but insightful. Yes, I can gradually change my irrational internal annoyance by creating better habits, but even before that, or while I'm doing it, I can exercise the virtue of prudence or practical wisdom. What this would mean is that, knowing my emotions are out of whack in being excessively annoyed, I can choose to remain silent, or be extra nice, or leave the situation, so that my actions don't hurt the person I'm annoyed with or contribute to my already bad habit. Maybe more universally, we should remember that virtue has to do with hitting the "mean," which in every case involves understanding a complex situation and doing the best available thing. When our emotions are out of whack, this kind of precision is pretty unlikely.

So under a certain lens, we can understand what Aristotle meant when he said that practical wisdom was in a sense all of virtue. When I'm exercising prudence, not only are my external actions what they would be if I had the virtue I'm missing, but even the internal pattern of virtue is somehow imitated by my soul. Externally, I'm nice to the guy I find annoying, but internally, my reason is guiding both my actions and my passions: my actions in the sense that I am treating the guy well, and my passions by not letting them take charge. On the other hand, practical wisdom alone can't be all of virtue absolutely speaking, because when I'm nice to somebody I find annoying, it hurts, and full virtue requires that good actions are done with pleasure. Of course, and maybe most importantly, acting thus according to prudence is the way to eventually gain the virtues I'm missing—it's the way to work toward actually liking the annoying guy. So understood in different ways, practical wisdom is an immediate shortcut to virtue, as well as a stepping stone toward gaining virtue in the long run.

It's important to note that one of the defining characteristics of practical wisdom is that it is *not* simply cleverness. A clever person is someone who can figure out the best way to get to some particular good. So an intelligent mafia boss or health insurance executive can be considered clever when they destroy human lives for personal profit. But they would not be considered prudent, because prudence is reasoning well with actions that contribute to the complete good of human life, which is immensely larger than financial gain, and includes the good of other people in our community (you can review all that in Book I). Practical wisdom is also not limited to cleverness, even in honest work, but includes it. It's not about just being a good mechanic or father or gardener, but being a good person and living a good life.

For all these reasons, practical wisdom is very difficult to gain and requires both practice and experience. This is the virtue you seek when you ask your grandmother for advice on life rather than your young physics professor, and even if she can't quite explain why her advice is best, more often than not it is. Among other reasons, she gives good advice because while she cares about you, she doesn't feel exactly what you're feeling, which means she can see things with a clearer head. You might be overly attached to certain things and your clouded judgment, especially in the moment, might cause you to make some big mistakes. This is why "sleeping on it" before making any important decision is always good advice, as well as avoiding being rushed into anything. Knowing this, gym coaches and car salesmen try their best to pressure you into signing a contract before the dust settles on their pitch and you realize you're getting ripped off. They also know that they should get you as excited as possible about the amazing fun that awaits you, because, as faithful Aristotelians, they realize that "pleasure destroys prudence." So to summarize all this, temperance is the best guarantee of prudence, but knowing about your own intemperance and not making decisions in the moment can save you a lot of heartache.

Politics

> "Perhaps one's own good cannot exist without household management, nor without a form of government." (VI.8)

Practical wisdom is a necessary virtue, among other reasons, because life is complicated. If life were simple, let's say if the whole point of our existence were to walk as far east as we could until we hit water, we wouldn't need much prudence, just a pair of legs and some Gatorade. As it is, our existence involves bodily health, nutrition, exercise, mental education, job competency, social interaction, family, friends, and an almost-infinity of other elements, each of which is itself unbelievably complex. Prudence is the virtue that helps us maneuver through each of these aspects of life, and orders them to each other, so that we know what's most important to a good life. It's no wonder that Aristotle thinks we can only learn it after a lot of experience.

Now take all that complexity and multiply it by every single person you know, and you'll have some idea how complex political life is. Then imagine someone thinking that an entire political regime with millions of people, each of them unbelievably complex beings and part of an unbelievably complex community, can be guided by a simple, universal ideology rather than by the virtue of political prudence. As a single individual, it would be idiotic for me to make a blanket rule that I should never give my money away. It would be equally idiotic to make a rule that I should always give it away. It just depends on the situation. But why should a country be guided by blanket rules like that, rather than an individual prudential response to each situation? The results of blanket-rule thinking are political ideologies such as libertarianism and totalitarianism. These are both opposites of prudence, since they simplify political life to the point of such abstraction that any actual contact with reality becomes offensive to them. That's why we end up hearing statements like "Well, if they can't afford medical treatment they should die—that's the Hand of the Market," and "Well, if you can't make your handrail exactly 28 inches above the floor like it says in the Code, you'll have to shut your business down." Ideology is the opposite of prudence and, therefore, the destruction of basic humanity. If the Sabbath was made for man, so much more economics and civil law.

An application of this, and a kind of microcosm of it, is family life. Living as part of a family and doing it well is a virtuous activity, which means it involves dealing with each complex person and situation in the appropriate way. It doesn't mean always applying the same rules or formulas, or always getting your way. "Happy wife, happy life" is as profound a bit of practical wisdom as anything in the *Nicomachean Ethics*. All the ideology in the world won't change the fact that you live with others, and their mood will affect your own. So living in a way that makes them also happy will in the end benefit you as well. The same goes for political communities and leadership: knowing how to live with people who disagree with you in a way that is mutually beneficial and enriching is central to political life, and is the fruit of the virtue of prudence. If not, if you just get your way to the detriment of everyone around you, you'll end up living the life of a tyrant, which is lonely and miserable.

Philosophical Life

"Not as the art of medicine produces health, but as health produces health . . . does philosophic wisdom produce happiness." (VI.12)

One last important idea before we move on to Book VII is a final reason why Aristotle brings up the intellectual virtues at all in his book on ethics, and it's an idea we've touched upon before. Human life is distinguished from the life of other things by the activity of thinking. So the intellectual virtues are in some way the most essentially human virtues, and the intellectual life is the most perfectly human life.

Before I explain what I think this means, here's what I don't think it means: I don't think living an intellectual life means living an academic life. I think an intellectual life is about being a thoughtful person, not about being a nerd. But "thoughtful" doesn't only mean "thoughtful of others." It means full of thought. So "philosophic wisdom" produces happiness in a different way than practical wisdom. Practical wisdom tells us where to drive or which friends to invite over; it helps us with decisions that will eventually help us and those around us. Philosophic wisdom produces happiness because it *is* happiness: it's not the decision to drive to the beach, it's the act of sitting and looking over the ocean; it's not the choice of which friends to invite over, it's the joyful conversation we have with them.

In a way, all the other virtues are just prerequisites for this kind of thoughtful living. If we are intemperate, our addictions to bodily pleasures distract us from this kind of awareness of life. If we are cowardly, or constantly pissed off, or obsessed with making money or people liking us, we're clogging up our minds with junk instead of the peaceful contemplation of reality that they're meant to have. And if we've been living that way our whole life, the habits that we've gained over all that time need to be understood before they're changed. So let's go on to Book VII.

Greek Word	English Approximation	Definition
nous	intuition	apprehension of first principles and concrete particulars
episteme	science	demonstrative knowledge
sophia	wisdom	*nous + episteme*
phronesis	prudence/practical wisdom	knowledge of the means toward living a good life
techne	art	knowledge of making
logos	reason	any of the above

Greek words for some reason

— Book VII —

Habits

In This Chapter:

Self-control, inner turmoil, being weak, feeling good.

Continence and Incontinence: Not Just about Peeing Your Pants

> "We must now discuss incontinence and softness, and continence and endurance; for we must treat each of the two neither as identical with virtue or wickedness, nor as a different genus." (VII.1)

Let me begin by introducing you to Some Dudes:

Some Dude number 1 is what you might call a rotten bastard; not only does he emotionally abuse his wife, he doesn't think what he's doing is wrong, and doesn't feel bad for it.

Some Dude number 2 is a drinker, and gradually getting worse. He hates hangovers though, and every time he goes to the bar, he promises himself he'll stop after the second drink. He just never does.

Some Dude number 3 just quit cigarettes a week ago. He hasn't had a single puff since then, but he really craves one.

Some Dude number 4 finally got to the point where he looks forward to his daily jog.

Each of these Dudes is in a different condition related to each of the other Dudes. But the condition of each Dude is determined not by his relation to the other Dudes, but by his relation to himself. More specifically, the condition of each Dude can be described by his relationship to his own actions and his own feelings. Here is a chart comparing each Dude, but using Aristotle's terminology rather than the word "dude":

Condition	Mind	Choice	Feeling
1. Vice	Bad	Bad	Bad
2. Incontinence	Good	Bad	Bad
3. Continence	Good	Good	Bad
4. Virtue	Good	Good	Good

The road to virtue

Yes, I'm boldly declaring that wife-beating is bad and jogging is good. If you disagree, plug in things you think are bad or good. If you still don't think anything can be bad or good, feel free to stop reading. I'm also declaring that someone's mind, choices, and feelings can also be good or bad, which is a little more complicated, but not very.

A **mind** is good that understands what's right in whatever the scenario is. Dudes 2–4 can all think straight: they know what's better and worse for themselves. Dude 1 can't even do that, and is convinced in his mind that hurting his wife is okay.

A **choice** that is good is one that follows a good mind. Dudes 3 and 4 know what they're supposed to do, and they do it. Dude 2 knows, but can't help himself when the bourbon hits his palate.

A **feeling** that is good is one that follows a good mind and a good choice. Dude 4 not only knows and does what's right; he enjoys it. Dude 3 does the right thing, but he still really wants to have that delicious menthol.

The goal for all of us is to become like Dude 4: to *know* the right thing, to *do* it, and to *have fun* doing it. This goes against what some of us grew up believing: that the more we suffer internally doing good things, the better we are as people. It turns out that this is what is commonly called "Extremely Wrong." We suffer when we improve, yes, because we're attached to dumb stuff that we shouldn't want. But the better we become, the more we enjoy being good. Remember: virtue is about happiness. Anything else is a bunch of passive-aggressive martyr-complex garbage.

It's worth saying that according to Aristotle, who seems to me to be right, the majority of us fit in the middle of the chart—we're mostly either continent or incontinent, Dude 2 or 3. Not a lot of people are totally vicious, who don't even believe wrong is wrong anymore (though plenty of people are confused, which is a different thing). And very few people are totally virtuous, and never have to struggle to do the right thing. Even rarer are two other Dudes that I didn't even put on the chart: Some Dude 0, whom Aristotle calls "beastly," and who takes intense pleasure in inhumanly horrible activities (someone like a serial killer or country music fan); there's also Some Dude 5, called "godlike," who is so virtuous that he seems inhumanly perfect. Let's leave these extremes behind and figure out how to get from Dude 1 to Dude 4.

You're Worse Than Ignorant

> "Socrates was entirely opposed to the view in question, holding that
> there is no such thing as incontinence; no one, he said, when he judges
> acts against what he judges best—people act so only by reason of
> ignorance." (VII.2)

Let's say you miss an anniversary. The next morning, you gradually begin to notice something is off with your spouse: a tone of voice, an extra moment of silence, the packing of bags, the sharpening of knives. Soon you have the good sense to ask what's wrong. Half an hour later, if you're still alive, you might, in the height of your depravity, utter the phrase "but I didn't intend to hurt you." Game over.

If you intend to hurt someone, that is an act of violence or malice. But not intending to hurt someone doesn't make you a saint. You didn't forget on purpose, or knowingly, as if that were somehow possible. But you forgot. Doing so unintentionally doesn't mean you're not selfish. It only means that your selfishness isn't intentional but habitual.

Aristotle cites Plato who cites Socrates who asked the question whether it's possible for someone to knowingly hurt themselves. The answer of Socrates, according to Plato, according to Aristotle, is no. The only way someone could hurt themselves is out of ignorance. But all wrongdoing, if you think about it, is a kind of self-harm. Therefore, says Socrates, all wrongdoing is done out of ignorance.

Aristotle doesn't agree—or at least he doesn't entirely agree. His evidence against Socrates is that all of us observe people doing things they know are bad for them all the damn time. This includes ourselves. Not two nights ago, I made the conscious decision to order, buy, and consume double the fast food I should have, knowing very well I would regret it later. In what way did I act in ignorance?

On the other hand, Aristotle argues that it is a *kind of* ignorance when we act in this way. He has a few different ways of analyzing this, and I'm not sure he settles on just one. Maybe (this may have been Plato's analysis) what I had two days ago was not knowledge but opinion about how much I should eat, and because I only had opinion, which is a weaker kind of thinking, that opinion caved in and disappeared when I got hungry. Maybe if it were real knowledge, it would have held up, or if I had a stronger character, my opinions would have more staying power in the face of the mighty temptation of White Castle (I think Socrates talks about this in *Republic* III, 413a-e).

Aristotle offers a different possibility. Maybe I had universal knowledge, but failed to apply it to a particular case. When you forgot your anniversary, someone could have asked you whether it's wrong for someone to forget an anniversary, and you would have said yes. That universal knowledge (about "someone") was there in your mind. What you failed to do is apply it to your particular case ("today is *my* anniversary"). Somewhat similarly, you might have had knowledge in what Aristotle calls "first actuality," ("my anniversary is May 13th"), but not had it in "second actuality," where you consciously think of the fact that your anniversary is May 13th, on May 13th. You can know something but not consciously think about it.

The reason why I like both Plato and Aristotle's explanations is that they both open the door to fault. Sure, you didn't think about the fact that today was your anniversary. But *why* didn't you think about it? I didn't think about my later regret when I ordered too much food. But *why* didn't I think about that, when it was exactly the thing I *should* have been thinking about? Because something *caused* me to be distracted, namely, my hunger. And you forgot your anniversary because something less important caused you to be distracted, because maybe you're a little more selfish than you admit.

This obviously isn't the case in every scenario, but I think it's common enough that most of us recognize it. One cause of "ignorance" or "forgetting" can easily be a strong feeling. Don't be naive about your emotions. People of the same species as you have forgotten that they love their husbands, their wives, their parents, or their kids, while under the influence of emotion, and destroyed more lives than just their own. So this kind of ignorance, according to Aristotle, is more like drunkenness than it is like illiteracy. In other words, the way you feel can affect the way you think, and the way you think can affect the way you feel. Which means we're right back to the question of training the passions.

Endurance and Softness

"While to the incontinent man is opposed the continent, to the soft is opposed the man of endurance." (VII.7)

Pleasure and pain are, physiologically, different things—there are pain receptors, but not pleasure receptors; there are different parts of the brain for each of them. At least that's what I vaguely remember hearing and I don't feel like looking it up. But soulwise, we're not talking only about physical pain and pleasure, but emotional as well. Even though Aristotle says that continence and incontinence primarily have to do with the same things that the virtue of temperance is about (that is, food and sex), he also says that there is an extended sense that applies to all kinds of pleasures. So it's possible for our reason to be clouded and our choice bossed around by all kinds of things. My example earlier about video games was an example of that.

Along the same lines, pain can be seen as a relative kind of thing. While there is a tangible, physical pain in plucking out a nose hair, there's also a kind of pain when we don't get the raise we're hoping for, or our internet dies out on us. And just like pleasure can have an effect on both our choices and our reason, pain of any kind can act the same way. When pain stops you from doing what you had chosen to do before, like a hangover making you change your mind about a morning workout, Aristotle calls it "softness." When you make it to the gym despite the pain, it's called "endurance."

Endurance is important because changing our habits is painful due to our attachments. Letting go of things hurts, and endurance is what allows us to keep going even when we're hurting. Because of that, endurance is a kind of prerequisite for continence, which in turn is a prerequisite for virtue. We have to be able to live with some pain if we're going to be able to live without some pleasure, if we're eventually going to be able to learn to take pleasure in something better. This seems to be a fundamental principle in changing our habits.

I remind you that not all pain is the same—even emotionally speaking. Some of it is caused by excessive attachment to stuff that isn't that important, and that kind of pain needs to be broken through and walked off. Some pain, however, is caused by trauma and internal injury, and needs to be dealt with and healed, and that is a topic that Aristotle doesn't address in this book. But it's important to know that there's a difference between the ache of a muscle that's new to exercise and an injury that needs to be tended to before you can get back to the gym. And knowing which pain you're feeling might not always be easy, so it's good to talk to people who can help you figure it out. Just not me, because I'm busy.

What that means is that sometimes stopping to figure out what your pain is about isn't "soft," but necessary, and that gritting your teeth and fighting through some pain might not be endurance but ignorance, and it might do way more harm than good. On the other hand, we're pretty good at making excuses for ourselves when we don't want to do something. Like I said, this isn't always easy to figure out. Welcome to ethics.

Transformation

"We are ready to pardon him if he has resisted." (VII.7)

This is probably the most important thing in this book. How do you get from vice to virtue? How do you improve your habits? One thing we know already is that you don't leapfrog. If you're incontinent, you generally don't become immediately virtuous. If you hate working out, you won't (without something like a miracle) suddenly enjoy it; if you're a heavy smoker, you won't suddenly hate it. This isn't magic, and if you're waiting until you feel like it, you'll be waiting forever. The whole reason why you have the bad habit you have is because you don't feel like changing, and you keep following your feelings. Incontinence needs to become continence before it becomes virtue: you need to exercise even when you don't want to—maybe especially then; you need to quit smoking even though you still like it. But I'm getting ahead of myself.

Let me put it confusingly. Newton's second law, F=ma, says that force and acceleration are proportional. So if you want to move something, you have to push. The bigger the force, the bigger the acceleration. But without a force, there won't be any change in velocity. So if you're floating or sitting around, don't expect anything to change without some effort. And the deeper the habit you're trying to change (let's say it's symbolized by "m" in the equation above), the greater the effort needs to be to change it.

One effort won't do, though. What we're trying to change isn't a single action but a *habit*. So trying super hard to do something different one day might get you moving, but it won't make a difference in the long run unless you maintain it. You're much better off trying a small but increasing bit of effort every day. If you're learning guitar, frantically practicing for eight hours once every six months won't make you a guitarist. Fifteen minutes a day will. In fact, with physical activities, a huge effort out of nowhere could injure you. If you've never done sprints or squats in your life and you do them for a half hour one day, you're not gonna be moving for a while after that. So start small, but keep up the effort. A little bit of force every day. And that means real effort, not coasting.

But each step in improving is a little bit different, because the thing you're trying to change is different. A vicious person, whose reason is enslaved, needs to start there and get in the habit of thinking clearly. That might mean doing some reading or talking to a friend, or talking themselves through a moment of darkness. It might even mean hitting rock bottom and having an epiphany kind of realization. Once their eyes open, they're no longer vicious, but incontinent. Now they know they aren't living the right way, but are too weak to stop. Not much better, but it's something.

An incontinent person needs to focus on their choices and actions. Dragging yourself out of bed even when it hurts; refusing that cigarette; consciously controlling your tone of voice. Little but consistent efforts, even when it hurts, and especially when it hurts. I challenge you to try it for a month. More likely than not, at the end of that month, it will at least hurt less. And if that trajectory continues, your good habit is on its way to being formed. And if you're trying to pick up a good habit, I suggest getting it over with in the morning rather than pushing it off to later in the day when you know very well it'll never happen.

A continent person, who does the right thing but doesn't enjoy it, has a different focus. Here you're not smoking but you still crave it; you're exercising but you hate it. The daily effort here, while maintaining the good choices you're used to, is more about your feelings than your actions. Here you should let yourself feel more fully, whereas when you were moving from incontinence you needed to grit your teeth to get things done. Believe it or not, fresh air without tar in your lungs feels pretty good, and so does a good workout. Now that you're here, let yourself enjoy it. The more you savor the good place you're at, the more attached you'll become, and the more you'll ingrain your habit to become a permanent part of yourself. Then, when you take pleasure in making the right choices, you'll be repulsed by the idea of doing anything else. That's a good place to be, but it takes time and patience, and daily effort, to get there. In fact, it also takes good friends, but that's the topic of the next two Books.

I think here we're in the best place to see why the idea of altruism can be so deceptive. Altruism is where you supposedly do something only for others, and not at all for yourself. But if you do something good and enjoy it, then that good thing is partially for you. So is it a worse act now that you enjoy it? Are you a less moral person if you take pleasure in helping others? And if you hated it but still did it, does that make you more moral? Some would say yes. And they would be wrong.

You feel pain doing good things when you're continent, and in that state, it makes sense to do something good despite the pain. But the pain doesn't add to the goodness of the act. It's only there to be overcome, and when you overcome it, move the hell on and enjoy your life. Carry your cross (in Christian language) and then when your sin dies, rise again and live with joy, to whatever degree you can in your life. There's no reason why a good thing shouldn't be good for you and for the person you're helping. The more things there are like that, the better it is for everyone.

Stubbornness

"The people who are obstinate are the opinionated, the ignorant, and the boorish—the opinionated being influenced by pleasure and pain; for they delight in the victory they gain if they are not persuaded to change." (VII.9)

An important aspect of habits, one that helps us even define what they are, is that they are persistent. Picking your nose, or smoking, or playing piano, are habits when they are difficult to get rid of. If you only picked your nose once and then stopped, or only smoked for a few weeks, or haven't played piano for years and forgot a lot of it, you don't have a habit. The thing that both good and bad habits have in common is that they are stubborn. That's why bad habits are so hard to get rid of, and good habits are so hard to gain. But good habits, once gained, are also persistent. So that's good I guess. Even though I'm pretty sure bad habits are way easier to gain, and I can't really give a non-religious reason as to why.

There is a difference between habits and stubbornness, though. A virtuous person would habitually refuse to do something they think is wrong, so they have a kind of stubbornness that's a good thing. But someone who is simply stubborn doesn't refuse to do something wrong; they refuse to change their mind even when they know they're wrong. Aristotle describes stubborn people as having a kind of intemperance, since they are somehow addicted to the pleasure of winning an argument, even if it goes against right reason. A virtuous person does the right thing no matter what the consequences; a stubborn person insists they are right whether or not they are. That's why it can be a vicious habit. The pleasure of winning has to be regulated by the truth, and a virtuous person would happily admit when they are proven wrong.

So when you make a decision to change a habit, be stubborn against yourself and your bad habits and feelings. That's the right place for stubbornness and even anger—they serve a purpose and this can be one of the purposes they serve. Be rigid when it comes to doing what's right. But be flexible when it comes to reason, and be ready to change your mind even when you don't want to.

Life Hurts

> "[Some pleasures] are pursued because of their intensity by those who cannot enjoy other pleasures. (At all events they go out of their way to manufacture thirsts somehow for themselves.). . . . For they have nothing else to enjoy and, besides, a neutral state is painful to many people because of their nature." (VII.14)

When I borrowed the video game last month (time really flies during quarantine), I made the choice to return it after a few days because I knew the damage it would do to my sleep schedule if I kept it. But even though that was painful, since the game was really fun, there was a worse alternative. I could have kept it and played it, and then gotten bored of it. Boredom might be the thing I fear most in life, and it's a sobering thing to realize that everything on earth eventually gets boring.

For a virtuous person, silly pleasures get boring pretty quickly, because virtuous people aren't silly enough to care much about them in the first place. But even deeper things become tiring, even having a great conversation with a good friend, which might be the deepest thing human life has to offer. This is because we need to eat and sleep and take breaks, and get our minds on different things, even if the thing we're thinking about is our favorite thing. Most doctoral students can testify to this, I think.

But for the rest of us, who aren't yet virtuous, it's even worse. Those of us who are unsettled and torn from within, whether through vice or incontinence, or through trauma and emotional hurt, have a hard time sitting still in the first place. Try it. Sit quietly in your room with no phone or computer or music playing. Just you existing. I'll be impressed if you can make it five minutes before your leg starts getting jittery. And again, it's not only because of trauma or a bad day. Even living in the state of continence or incontinence means there's a division within you, a war between what you know is right and what you want to do, and that war alone is painful.

So for a lot of us, life itself, far from being pleasant, kind of hurts. And instead of addressing the pain in a healthy way, very often we distract ourselves with anything we can. But the pain stays, so we have to keep distracting ourselves (this is called "diversion" by Blaise Pascal, who is a lot smarter than I am). We jump from bar to bar, concert to concert, drug to drug, job to job, workday to workday, cowboy boot to cowboy boot. The noise or the lights or the orgasm or the paycheck feels good and then it's gone, because just like video games, it gets boring. Then the pain starts sneaking up again, and the music, the drugs, or the paycheck, has to get bigger and louder and more intense to block it out. Imagine you have a bleeding wound in your leg, but instead of cleaning and bandaging it, you just get drunk so you don't feel it. It will never heal that way, and if anything it will get infected. That's how a lot of us spend a lot of our lives. Self-destruction because it feels better than sitting still.

Real Pleasure

> "This is why it is not right to say that pleasure is perceptible process, but it should rather be called activity of the natural state, and instead of 'perceptible,' 'unimpeded.'" (VII.12)

Let's say you're doing some awful unnatural activity like walking outside. And let's say it's under some horrible circumstances, like it's sunny. So the sunlight is literally hitting your head. When you're in that much pain, even the simple relief of some shade feels good. This is what Aristotle would call "restorative" pleasure. It's the good feeling we get when pain is taken away.

But now let's say you're in the shade somewhere, and on top of that, you just had a good meal, washed your hands, caught up with work, and talked your friend out of buying skinny jeans. Things are good. Life is good. You close your eyes and you feel the breeze blow through your elegant salt-and-pepper beard. That feels good too, but it's not "restorative." It just feels good. It's plain old pleasure.

Aristotle has a tough time giving a definition of pleasure. In one spot, he describes it as "unimpeded activity," meaning there's nothing internally or externally in the way of you doing what you want to do, like closing your eyes during the breeze. But it's not exactly the act of closing your eyes. It's something that goes along with it—in Aristotle's words, it's something that "accompanies" a good activity.

Why talk about this at the end of the chapter on developing habits? Because the virtuous state is exactly the one where there's nothing within us impeding our good activity. When we've attained virtue, we can act with all our souls undivided, reason, will, and feeling. And activity that's like that feels good. That's the kind of activity that pleasure "accompanies."

You can see already that this is a different thing than the simply bodily enjoyment of food or sex. Pleasures like these do accompany an activity, but in many cases (like when we eat or sex too much or with the wrong person or something), the activity doesn't follow reason, so there's division within the soul, and therefore an obstacle. The activity isn't "unimpeded." When the whole soul is united, even bodily pleasures become more pleasant. Probably.

But what about other activities? Aristotle seems to be thinking about a master musician playing her favorite song. In situations like that, the activity of playing is so unified, the focus of the musician is so intense, that her pleasure in playing becomes infectious, and her audience, in their own activity of listening to her, gets to share in her joy. This kind of shared happiness isn't a side issue—it seems to be absolutely fundamental to human life, according to Aristotle. That's why, I think, he dedicates the next two Books of the *Ethics* to the topic of friendship.

But before that, there's a lot to contemplate about this kind of pleasure. Even without the audience, the musician I described is doing something pleasant for herself. She has worked for years, with discipline and self-sacrifice, to be able to do what she's doing, and her playing is no longer a chore; it's no longer "practice;" it's now really "playing"—it's fun. You see the same in great athletes and great scholars, great teachers, great counselors, great parents, great welders and mechanics and writers and readers. I think just by knowing what pleasure like this is about we learn a lot about what it is to be human. It's not about getting or gaining or receiving, but about doing, and doing so well that we do it joyfully. Becoming this kind of person with life itself is what ethics is all about.

Book VIII

Friendship

In This Chapter:

Needs, wants, friends, sharing, caring.

A Virtue

> "After what we have said, a discussion of friendship would naturally
> follow, since it is a virtue or implies virtue, and is besides most neces-
> sary with a view to living." (VIII.1)

I wonder what it means when Aristotle says that friendship is a virtue or implies virtue? Does that mean that there are vicious friendships? Or friendships that are continent or incontinent? Maybe one friend knows that the
friendship is harmful and needs to end, but is too attached to end it. Maybe
"implies virtue" means that in order to have real friendships, we need to
already have other virtues, like courage or generosity. Or it might mean the
opposite—that when we become friends, we learn courage or generosity.

   This is the kind of conversation that friends can have with each
other, and I think it's the kind of thing Aristotle would have done with
his friends. Don't get the wrong idea—you and I aren't friends, so do not

attempt to contact me under any circumstances, especially not to invite me on your podcast.

But there's an important point to be made as these two books on friendship begin—that friendship is "necessary with a view to living." Remember from Book I that human life is its own kind of thing—that it's not just about nutrition or sensation, but about reason. So friendship is necessary for that, not the non-human stuff. We can eat and look at stuff by ourselves, but, if Aristotle is right, we can't reason by ourselves; at least not very well. Logos, the Greek word for "reason," also means (among like fifty other things) "conversation." So in some real, fundamental way, what it means for us to reason well is to have a conversation, and if Aristotle is right about the necessity of friendship, it means having a conversation with someone else.

This is not a side issue, nor do I think the two Books on friendship are unrelated works stuck into the *Ethics* by a later editor. I really think that everything has been leading up to this. I think that all of ethics, the science of human happiness, is about friendship. That's why one-fifth of the book is dedicated to it, and maybe the most important fifth. Let's try to take it seriously when Aristotle says the dramatic things he says about friendship. He might be onto something.

The Need for Friends

"Without friends no one would choose to live, though he had all other goods." (VIII.1)

Making friends is hard work, just like any virtue is. And just like any virtue, becoming friends with someone is a little awkward at first and takes effort and practice until it becomes a part of you. But like all good things, a good friendship is worth the effort, and Aristotle spends a little time arguing why it's such a good thing. Not to make us sad if we don't have any (or many) friends, but to motivate us to put in the work to make them.

His conclusion, which he puts first like a high schooler with a thesis statement, is that *nobody would choose to live without friends*, even if they got everything else. As evidence, he gives examples about money, hardship, age, and the act of thinking I discussed in the last section.

If you're poor, having friends can help alleviate your poverty—not only in terms of gaining or borrowing money, but also in terms of making connections and gaining opportunities that you wouldn't have without those friends. I don't think Aristotle is here condoning favoritism towards your friends in the workplace. I think he's just recognizing a fact of life, for better or worse. More interestingly, if you're rich, friends are perhaps even more important, because it is friends that give value to money itself. What good is all that money if you don't have anyone to spend it with? Again, I think Aristotle isn't so much arguing for people splurging on the extra yacht instead of helping the poor, but just pointing out a fact of life. If anything (if I can anticipate something that will come up later), Aristotle seems to be working under the assumption that the more friendship is nourished, encouraged, and expanded, the better it is for the whole society. So it's not so much about justifying what rich people do with their money as showing them that friendship is better than all the money in the world.

If you're young, you have fun having fun, and having fun with friends is way more fun. But you also gain deeper things than fun: what you, as a stupid young person, lack, is wisdom, and you can gain that wisdom by having wiser friends (I think maybe something like a mentor). If you're old, you need help getting around and getting things done, and you're also looking back on a long life wondering what to do with all the experience you've gained. A younger friend can help you get things done, and can offer a grateful ear to your wisdom. This is one model for the relationship between grandparents and grandchildren, and it's one that I've found enriching personally. However, if you're a young person and don't have the good fortune to have living or wise grandparents, visiting a retirement home and talking to anyone there for half an hour would be a better use of your time than almost anything else (including reading this book), and it would cheer someone up for a month.

For everyone though, Aristotle moves from these particular cases to a general case, and this helps him move toward establishing his thesis statement quoted at the start of this section. It's not only the poor or rich, the young or old, or any other category of person whose lives are improved by the addition of friends. It's human beings just considered in their humanity. Friends do not simply improve poverty or old age, or wealth or youth. They improve life itself, and the very reality of being human. That is because of something he has yet to prove but he has mentioned already: *friends help you be a human being*, which means they help you act well and think well. There's a lot to say about this later, but for now I'll give you a hint: remember that acting virtuously means acting according to both reason and feeling, and when you do something for a friend, it's a lot easier to do it because you care about them.

Who Is My Friend?

"A parent seems by nature to feel [friendship] for offspring and offspring for parent[,] . . . it is felt mutually by members of the same race[;] . . . we may see even in our travels how near and dear every man is to every other." (VIII.1)

Virtues are built on natural tendencies—remember that some people are naturally brave or generous, and have a bit of a head start with those virtues when they begin to develop them. Friendship, like any other virtue, is built on natural affection. There are certain people that, for one reason or another, you just get along with better. These natural feelings of affinity are a good foundation for a good friendship.

The alternate idea is to attempt to be friends, immediately and in the same way, with everyone. This is a beautiful idea—even to love your enemies—but it's not meant to be taken in isolation (or at least I don't think it is). We can't immediately cause ourselves to be friends with, or love, or even like, all of humanity, as if it were a simple act of the will to do so. Kindness is a choice, but friendship (because it's a virtue) is a habit, which means it has to grow gradually. Kindness is also (mostly) external, which means we can be kind to people we can't stand. But friendship, like any virtue, really does involve the emotions, which means we can only be true friends with people we like. An old saying goes, you should love everyone, but you don't have to like them.

An all-encompassing friendship to humanity, if it's at all possible, cannot therefore be a strained or forced decision on your part. To the extent that it's possible at all, it needs to be an extension of the natural friendship you have with those close to you. Plato's *Republic* mentions a "noble lie" wherein citizens of a country are told that they are all siblings, which is supposed to make them care about each other. But the lie becomes obvious, and brotherly affection wears off when there are thousands of siblings around. It would be much better, says Aristotle, to be a second cousin in reality than a brother in the way Plato says.

I think Aristotle is right. I don't think affection for what's yours (whether your friends, your family, your city, or your country) is in opposition to caring about the whole world or the whole human race, as if loving humanity meant loving your own family less. On the contrary, your family, friends, and city, are places to nurture your own heart and care for others so that you can expand, little by little, to others as well.

This seems to me to be politically very wise. When it's just you and the world, there's not really any reason you should want to care about the world. But when you have a family that you care about, that means you have a stake in the school board of your city and the laws of your country, which means you feel the need in your very blood to get out and make things better for everyone. It's naive to think cutting the roots of love within family will lead to more love for humanity. There isn't some quantified bucket of "friendship" that is distributed and therefore used up by family or city or nation. Friendship is rather a living thing that grows from one to the other. Cut off the root and you don't expand it, you destroy it.

Definition of Friendship

"Goodwill when it is reciprocal [is] friendship. Or must we add 'when it is recognized'?" (VIII.2)

There are three parts to Aristotle's definition of friendship (yes, he probably didn't have many friends if he spent his time trying to figure out the definition of friendship). There's goodwill, reciprocality, and recognition.

Goodwill means caring about someone's well being—literally willing something good for them. The different kinds of "good" that you can will for someone are distinguished in the next section, but here it's enough to say that you are a friend to someone when, first of all, you want good things for them and not bad ones. Of course, the third alternative, that you don't care at all, is certainly not friendship either. So it's an active concern for someone else's well being, not just because of what they can do for you, but because of who they themselves are.

Other virtues approach friendship in their own way, but don't quite make it. Generosity is concerned with doing good for others, as are justice and basically all the moral virtues. But when a generous person is generous, while his generosity benefits others, the main beneficiary is he himself, since giving is a better thing than receiving. And of course this is just fine—remember that this whole ethics deal is fundamentally about finding your own happiness. But with friendship, your pleasure is not in the good you do as a virtuous act contained within you, but in the good of your friend, who is outside you. So if there's any "altruistic" element in Aristotle's understanding of ethics, it's here. You feel joy when good happens, and pain when bad happens, to them and because of them, not because of you. When a friend loses a beloved parent, your sadness isn't because they'll be busy and not able to see you for a while because of funeral arrangements. You're sad just because something sad happened to them. When they finally got that book deal they've worked at for years, you're not happy because they can finally stop complaining about how irritating publishers are to deal with, like they own the freaking world. You're happy just because they are.

The next part, that a friendship must be *reciprocal*, is extremely important. If you have this habit of action and feeling toward someone and they do not have it toward you, that is something other than a friendship. It could be stalking, or emotional slavery, but if it's one-sided it isn't friendship. This makes an important point: without some form of self-esteem (maybe related to what Aristotle called "magnanimity" earlier), friendship becomes impossible. You have to first be a friend to yourself (love your neighbor *as yourself* assumes you love yourself first). If one of you is pusillanimous or without self-esteem, or a narcissist incapable of really caring about others as themselves rather than useful tools, that is neither friendship nor virtue.

The last part, that a friendship is reciprocal goodwill that is *recognized*, is also important, and not just for obvious reasons. The obvious part is that it would be weird if two people cared about each other equally but neither one knew of the other's goodwill. It's certainly something that could happen, but it would be weird to call that a friendship. But the recognition or awareness of one another's goodwill is even more essential than that, for reasons that will be brought out in the next Book. For now, just remember again that thoughtful awareness is not just some random thing that humans do, but is the defining factor of humanity. And if a friend can be a part of that, then friendship cuts to the core of being human.

Figure 8: The definition of friendship

Kinds of Goods and Friends

"There are therefore three kinds of friendship, equal in number to the things that are lovable." (VIII.3)

"Reciprocalness" and "recognition" are fairly clear terms, and generally carry the same sense whenever used (though a thing can be unequally "reciprocal"). But "goodwill" can have more than one meaning, since "good" can have more than one meaning. When I "will" a "good" for a friend, what exactly does that mean? Aristotle boils it down to three different—not just distinct—things, and these three good things that we can will for each other end up distinguishing the three kinds of friendship. You might remember that these different goods were discussed all the way back in Book I, but if you don't that's fine.

The first kind of good we can will for someone is *a material good*. I want someone to have financial success, and he wants the same for me, and we are somehow in that mutual willing together, and recognize that fact. This might best be called a "partnership" more than a "friendship," since that's what it's really about. Financial or professional success, and nothing more, being willed for someone in a reciprocal way just means being business partners of one kind or another. This, Aristotle recognizes, is barely a friendship, though it's possible to also be friends in one of the other two senses with someone you also happen to work with.

Aristotle's term for this first one (at least in a typical English translation) is a friendship of "utility," but I think "partnership" works just fine. But to understand why it's "barely" a friendship we need to understand the kind of good being willed. Material goods, including money, can certainly be divided and distributed, and hopefully with fairness. But they can't be shared. If you and your partner make $500 one month, and you're equal partners, you each get $250 (minus taxes). You don't both get the $500, which is what "sharing" really means. Business partnerships, or friendships of utility, don't share, they divide. But still, you each want one another to be successful, since that's a good thing for both of you, so it's still a good thing in itself. It's just not much of a friendship.

The second kind of good is *pleasure*. It's a big step up from money, and the friendship based on it is also a big step up, because pleasure is the kind of thing that really can be shared. When you're watching a comedy with a friend who has a similar sense of humor, your laughter becomes contagious—Jack Black does something funny, and then you laugh, and then your friend laughs, and then you notice your friend laughing, and he notices you, and you both laugh harder. Something similar happens when you share a meal. You try the appetizer, and then you say "Wow! Try these fried brussels sprouts with bacon and parmesan that we're eating with weird forks because we're at a hipster restaurant in a recently gentrified neighborhood." Then your friend tries them and says, "Wow! You're right, that is unusually salty," which causes you to think about the saltiness and savor it even more. The pleasure in these cases, unlike the money above, multiplies when it's shared, and the more your friend or friends enjoy what you're enjoying, the more you enjoy it, because you enjoy the fact that they're enjoying it too. I guess the same thing goes for sex probably.

Remember that these types of friendships are defined by their maximum. A work partnership is one that is *at most* concerned with material goods, and a friendship of pleasure is one that is *at most* concerned with having fun together, though you can have fun with work partners, which would, especially in those instances, make them more than just work partners. Similarly a friendship of pleasure can be incorporated into the third kind of friendship, which Aristotle calls a "true" friendship or a friendship of virtue.

You can get an idea of why a true friendship is different than a mere friendship of pleasure by thinking about the good that the friends wish for one another. A friend of pleasure wishes pleasure for the other, and wishes to share in that pleasure, whereas a true friend wishes not only pleasure but *all good things*, and especially *the best things*, for the other. The difference can be seen when the pleasure (or, in the case of the work partnership, the money) is taken away. Let's say you lose a loved one and are in mourning. You're not able, for many reasons, to have fun with your friend in the same way while you're feeling like this. A friend of only pleasure wouldn't know, or care to know, what to do with you. A true friend, however, isn't your friend just for the fun but also for the bad times like this. Even if it's sad (the literal opposite of fun), your friend will be with you and share your sadness in whatever way they can, see if you need help with funeral arrangements, talk you through the dark thoughts, or just sit with you quietly when you don't want to be alone. Nothing fun, or profitable, about any of that. Of course they'll also be there when you're ready to have fun or make money again, but the friendship isn't built on those things, so it's there when those things aren't.

This is also called a friendship of virtue because virtue is a great thing to wish for another, and a very different thing than pleasure. It's pretty easy to imagine how the two can come into conflict, and I bet a lot of you have experienced this difference in your group of friends. Some friends want the fun and games, even if those fun and games are harmful or destructive, or a waste of time, or building a bad habit. These are friends of pleasure only. Other friends want what's best, and if having a little less fun means having a hangover-free morning, they're willing to sacrifice the fun for the greater good, and to challenge you to do the same, even if it makes you upset at them. That's not a fun place to be as a friend, but sometimes it's important when the friendship is a true one.

There are different models or patterns of virtuous friendships that we can imagine. One, that I think Aristotle had in mind in some places, is that between a mentor and a student. Even though the goods aren't equally distributed (the mentor gives more than he receives, at least in one way), what is wished for the other is knowledge or virtue, not just fun or profit. A friendship of virtue that is equal is (or should be) that between spouses, people who share all of life together, distinguished from mere sexual partners or one-night stands which are interested only in pleasure. Spouses with this kind of friendship stick together even when the other is in need, or when the fun and games are over and life gets serious.

Giving and Getting

> "But [friendship] seems to lie in loving rather than being loved, as is
> indicated by the delight mothers take in loving." (VIII.8)

I talked earlier about self-esteem (somewhere in Book IV?) and it's important to remember that virtues, including that of friendship, are meant to
be mutually-supportive rather than contradictory: being just isn't opposed
to being brave or temperate, but all of them (when rightly understood and
applied) go together. So when we talk about the kind of love we're to have
toward our friends, other virtues are still being assumed, including the kind
of healthy self-love that's implied in the virtue of magnanimity. When one
is taken in isolation from the other, relationships can be much more destructive than virtuous.

That said, self-centeredness is not the same as self-esteem, and as a
vice it's particularly poisonous toward the virtue of friendship. I've also noticed that it's often caused by low self-esteem. For example, obsessing over
which of your friends asks about you or checks in to see how you are, and
being hurt when they don't, and taking tabs on when they do and when
they forget, is developing a habit that could become really unhealthy. If the
friends in question are truly neglectful and uncaring, then it might be time
to make some new ones. But if they aren't, the problem might be you, not
them, and you might be seeing things only because you're looking for them.

In any case, what you're doing isn't what friendship is about. Friendship isn't about what you get, but what you give. But that greeting-card sentence isn't as empty as it seems. Remember that friendship is a virtue (or
implies virtue), so it's related to habits of thoughts, actions, and feelings. So if
friendship is about what you give, that means what you think, do, and enjoy
is focused on your friend, not yourself, when you're exercising the virtue
of friendship. It means you're happiest when you get to make them happy.
When they do something for you, that's also nice, but it takes second place.
Not in a weird repressive passive-aggressive "Oh, you didn't have to do this"
way, but really and truly. And if you're not quite there, that only means you
need to work on this virtue some more. Now imagine two friends both having this virtue, and finding their greatest happiness in making one another
happy. Now imagine a society where there's lots of that.

Aristotle's example is interesting, because he uses it to focus on the virtue itself. Remember that happiness is an activity, not a passively received

thing. So the activity of the virtue of friendship is not passive either (which is just what I've been saying in this section). The model for this virtue is a friend who gives without any thought of what is given back, and the best example that Aristotle can think of is the mother of a child. In this scenario, the mother gives enormously of her time and energy to a little weird being who is so helpless that he or she can't be imagined to give anything back in return. But the idea (which certainly isn't always the case, but is hopefully there a lot of the time) is that the mother doesn't need anything in return—her joy is simply in giving to her child.

I repeat that this virtue takes other virtues for granted, and that caring for someone else in this way requires you to care also and primarily for yourself. But that doesn't change the fact that there is a real and beautiful joy that comes simply from giving and caring about someone else. This particular type of joy is the essence of friendship.

Hard to Get

"But it is natural that such friendships should be infrequent, for such men are rare." (VIII.4)

Don't feel too bad if you haven't experienced this very much. It's possible that you're not quite virtuous enough to do it (remember that friendship might imply virtues that you might not yet have), and it's also possible that you haven't found friends capable of receiving it. The prerequisites for this kind of activity are pretty intense: you have to be good (which means you have to have lots of virtues and maybe all of them), you have to know your goodness, your friend also has to be good and know it, and you each have to know each other's goodness. Why is that?

This all has to be there already because friendship is built on trust. There goes another greeting-card phrase, but again it's more interesting than you think. You can't give if you don't think you have anything good to give in the first place, so you have to have some trust in yourself. But you also can't give if the person receiving isn't good, or can't be trusted to receive openly. That's because giving is a vulnerable activity, and opens you up. If they don't receive, or receive badly, or take advantage of you, or hurt you when you give, that ruins the whole thing, and the activity isn't what it's meant to be. There's no joy in that, and only pain. And continuing in that kind of false friendship would require you to harm yourself, which goes against the prerequisite virtue of self-care.

The conclusion that Aristotle makes, which sounds really harsh, is that only good people can be friends in the true sense of the word. Two scoundrels can be work partners (and many are), and two jerks can be friends of pleasure and have fun together. But you can't have a true friendship unless you're good and your friend is good. One of the many reasons for this is that true friends don't just love the same thing but each other, and loving something that isn't lovable is an injustice to yourself and a kind of self-deceit (with the obvious exception of loving someone who is bad but really working on it, which is itself lovable).

Think about the other virtues. If you're a coward, and your friend needs you to do something scary, you'll fail to do it. If you're intemperate, and distracted by some lust or another, you won't realize what your friend needs—you might not even notice your friend at all, but only see them as an object of your lust. If you're greedy, you will have trouble being generous enough to give even to friends. And so on with many, if not all, the virtues. And something similar happens not just with vice but even incontinence— maybe you're not a vicious coward, but if you know you're needed and cave in out of fear, that will still hurt your friends.

Don't be discouraged. First of all, everyone has their own struggles, and like I said earlier just knowing and working on your bad habits is a lovable thing and that alone can help you be a better friend to others (not surprisingly, at the same time it makes you a better friend to yourself). Second, and maybe most importantly, the deep need we all have to escape loneliness and have real friends is an important motivator for us to try and become better people.

In the end, though, this means that real friendship, or even two imperfect people striving for real friendship, is pretty rare. So if you have a handful of real friends, cherish them and don't expect many more (in fact, it's not really possible to have a ton of true friends, for reasons I'll discuss in the next Book). If you don't, don't be discouraged and keep trying, because it's worth the effort.

Community

> "All the communities, then, seem to be parts of the political community; and the particular kinds of friendship will correspond to the particular kinds of community." (VIII.9)

As usual, Aristotle points us from ethics to politics, since for him they are so connected that they're almost one and the same thing. Here the connection is pretty obvious: friendship is about connection, and so is politics. Yet again, the greeting-card phrase "friendship is about connection" has a more precise meaning than we think. Community isn't just a bunch of people living or feeding in the same place ("like cattle") but something real and intimate—it means living a human life together, which means something similar to friendship. The communion or connection between friends is that each of them wants what's good for the other, and takes pleasure in the other being happy. The communion of a city can't have that kind of direct intensity, but there is a similarity: what's good for the city is good for me, as a citizen. If my neighborhood gets a new library or fountain, or if our sports team wins, or if we elect a good mayor, that good thing for the city is something that I can be directly happy about, even if I never make it to the library or care about sports. That's because I share in the good of the city in the real sense of sharing that I discussed earlier. When the library or fountain is built, everyone gets to visit and see them, and that good isn't divided or lessened when more people go, but if anything, increased.

Aristotle closes this first Book on friendship by making a more detailed political analogy. I'm not quite sure if his main point is about friendship or about politics, but it's interesting either way. He says that this kind of sharing or connection can take on one of three different models: *monarchy*, *aristocracy*, or *polity*, and that each of these models can decay into a selfish version of itself, which are *tyranny*, *oligarchy*, and *democracy*.

In a true monarchy, the ruler is in charge but does what's best for the whole city, not just himself, the way (in Aristotle's analogy) parents take care of children, not only themselves. Of course, this can decay into selfishness and the king and the parents can turn into tyrants. Similarly, in an aristocracy, different jobs are assigned according to the particular strengths of the members of government, but all work together for the good of each other and the whole city; the analogy here is with husbands and wives dividing their duties to the family according to whatever each is good at, but caring for the whole family. Because the authority is still in a few hands, this can decay into an oligarchy, where the ruling class takes care only of itself, and neglects or uses the rest of the citizens for its own profit. A polity is governance where each member has an equal share, and all are invested in one another's good and care for the whole community, the way siblings are supposed to be (but never really are). Democracy (which Aristotle doesn't mean the same way we mean it) is when those who are equal care only about themselves and not the community as a whole.

I'm not exactly sure what the point of this analogy is, besides stressing that we, as friends and as citizens, should do all we can to focus on what we share with others rather than what's only our own, and that this is the one and only thing that separates a healthy friendship from a sick one, and a healthy city from a rotten one.

— Book IX —

More Friendship

In This Chapter:

Truth, self-care, making friends, good living.

Honesty

"The love of character endures because it is self-dependent." (IX.1)

Let's review the three types of friendship, or rather the one "true" friendship and the two "kind of" friendships. That of utility or business partnership has some material end; that of pleasure is about having fun together; that of virtue (or in the quote above, character) is the true one. The reason why only the third is a "true" friendship is, to say it more explicitly, only true friends really care about each other. Business partners care about the money; friends of pleasure care about the fun. But if you care about someone just for who they are, and they care about you in that way, you're true friends.

Make sure you and your friend are clear about what kind of friendship you have, because things can get awkward. Work friends who are only work friends inviting you to hang out after work are inviting you to transition to another kind of friendship. When you say "No thanks, that sounds like a nightmare," you're politely committing to continuing a friendship of utility with them. When your bar friends aren't there to help you move or grieve the loss of your beloved cat, don't be very surprised. They were only in it for the fun, and when the fun is gone, so are you. As long as all this is clear from the outset, nobody gets hurt.

Of course, what this means is that the most lasting kind of friendship is the friendship of virtue. Virtue is a habit, and habits are stable things, so a friendship built on that foundation can withstand a lot for a long time. But profit is based on values and stocks and other horrible things, and these horrible things are unstable things that can be affected by the wind or a virus. So a friendship built on them has about the same stability. The same thing goes for pleasure, both because most kinds of fun are unsustainable for a long time (at some point your body just begs you for no more hangovers), and because most kinds of fun get boring. So friendships based on fun have a similar lifespan. Again, know this going in and you won't be hurt.

But let them know as well, which means be honest not only about your intentions with the friendship, but about who you are. A friendship based on virtue needs to be based on something real, and if you pretend to be someone you're not, the friendship is based on an illusion, which means the friendship is an illusion. This is especially important in romantic relationships and marriages. If the relationship is more than just a weird "friends with benefits" thing, it falls into the category of a friendship of virtue or character. That means you really need to know each other, which means if one or both of you is being fake or dishonest, the relationship itself is a sham, and a lot of pain will follow.

Partiality

"We must for the most part return benefits rather than oblige friends." (IX.2)

What would you do if your best friend on earth, who went above and beyond in helping you through a rough time in life without asking for anything, needed you to break a promise you made to yourself that you'd never wear Axe Body Spray, and somehow his very life depended on you doing just that? Would you let him die before selling out your devotion to Brut Splash-On Cologne?

What if it wasn't your best friend on earth, but rather a guy that your cousin owes a favor to, whom you've kind of seen around? And what if it wasn't breaking your promise to yourself about Axe Body Spray, but instead he needed someone to drive the getaway car for his hilariously ill-thought-out bank robbery? And what if he didn't even need the money to survive, but was planning on blowing it on several crates of Axe Body Spray?

It's pretty obvious that you should say "Yes" to the first proposal and "No, you idiot" to the second. It's good to keep a promise, including one to yourself, but friendship has its own value, and there are times when it weighs more than promises like that. On the other hand, it doesn't weigh so much that a casual acquaintance should expect you to break the law for his sake.

These dumb examples illustrate that there is something justly owed simply to a friend as a friend, and that this duty to them is included within the overall picture of ethics. But as usual, the "in between" scenarios become more difficult to balance. Nepotism is obviously wrong and harmful, but what if your sister happened to be the most qualified applicant to the job you're hiring for? Should you *not* hire the best candidate? Or would that be unjust as well? On the other hand, is it fair for her to expect special treatment as your sister? There may be scenarios where that expectation is fair as well.

This is the typical complexity we've come to expect in ethics, and yet again it's the virtue of prudence that needs to do its job in figuring out the best course of action. Your alliances of utility, like an allegiance to a political party or business, do have some claim on you, but not to the detriment of your family or community, which are higher priorities. You owe your drinking buddies something, but not something that would hurt your spouse. Those examples are clear. But it's not clear whether you should invite all your mom's cousins to your wedding even if that means you don't have any room for your friends, or take sides in the argument between your husband and your dad, or sacrifice your daughter to appease the gods for the good of your kingdom. How all these different kinds of friendship relate to each other is a complicated thing, because they are social things, and like all social things it takes some experience and some finesse to figure them out. So do your best to be fair to everyone and even to make everyone happy, but realize that won't always be possible.

Aristotle discusses a special case of this in the situation where someone who was a close friend changes, and takes on bad or destructive habits. On the one hand, you owe it to yourself to protect yourself from possible harmful relationships; on the other hand, you owe something to your friend, even if they aren't the same person they were. Aristotle's answer seems to be that you should make a sincere and patient effort to help your friend become better. If they agree to this, you've done what's best both for yourself and for them. If not, at least you tried. If they agree but keep slipping, prudence again needs to kick in to figure out when and where and how to draw the line.

Friendship with Yourself

> "Friendly relations with one's neighbors, and the marks by which friendships are defined, seem to have proceeded from a man's relations to himself." (IX.4)

I may have already mentioned Aristotle's assertion that "a friend is another self." Aristotle moves back and forth between a healthy relationship with a friend and a healthy relationship with oneself, and I think both sides of this comparison are illuminating. He lists five attributes of friendship, some based on the definition he gave in Book VIII and some a touch more arbitrary but still pretty relatable. Then, after listing the five, he comes in with the "Ka-pow! These all apply to your relationship to yourself!" Rather than do that, I'll take each one in turn and apply it to both sides of the comparison. What we'll end up with is not just a good description of friendship but also of the ideas of healthy self-care, magnanimity, or self-esteem that we've touched upon a number of times already.

The first attribute is to wish and do good for the sake of the friend. When applied to yourself, this assumes a decent amount of virtue and wisdom—in order to do what's best for yourself, you have to know it, and in order to do what's best for yourself, you have to have some level of self-control in order to follow reason (which knows what's good) rather than passion (which can often have destructive attachments). I don't know how accurate it is to treat self-destructive behavior as some exceptional disorder—to some degree, most of us are self-destructive. At the time of this writing, for example, I've purchased the video game system that I couldn't handle a few chapters ago. I've justified it in terms of needing relaxation, but it's hard to know if I'm being biased. If it ends up being destructive again, and if I'm a real friend to myself, I'll need to at least moderate my use of it.

Something interesting occurs when we apply this attribute to a friend. We immediately run back into the question of what kind of "good" we wish for them, and the idea of the three goods of utility, pleasure, and virtue, come back to the forefront. This brings back, in stark relief, the differences between the three types of friendship, and the superiority of the third. I should want my friend to be a good person, and to find the kind of happiness that comes from that. Wanting only money or pleasure for them is to sell them short of the greater good that they're capable of. Now switch back to yourself, and do the same thing.

The second attribute is to want the friend to exist. I think this is more fundamental than the first one, even though Aristotle lists it second (probably because the first one is a close restatement of his definition). This one hits hard on the ol' self-esteem. Are you glad that *you* exist? In my experience with myself and a lot of others, this might not be as crystal clear as we'd hope, which I think is one reason Aristotle lists it. I think for many people, the answer depends on their mood, or the kind of day they had, or the part of their soul that you're asking. While instinct seems for the most part to push us toward survival, the explicit, conscious, positive desire to exist might be elusive sometimes, and more a matter of habit and practice than of some indestructible aspect of our nature. Hang in there, bud.

When applied to a friend, this reveals something interesting. Are you positively, consciously happy that your friend exists, or do you tolerate their existence because there's nothing else to do, and nobody better around to be friends with? If it's the latter, you might consider reconsidering things, and trying to build a habit of deeper appreciation for them. I have a feeling that doing this might help you grow in appreciation of your own existence.

The last three attributes that Aristotle lists can be grouped together: living/sharing life with your friend, having similar tastes, and grieving and rejoicing with them. The basic idea in all three is that of harmony and getting along. When applied to yourself, this becomes nothing other than a description of the virtuous state of the soul: what it means for you to be virtuous is to be at harmony with yourself rather than divided, your mind and your feelings living together, wanting the same things, and feeling pleasure and pain at the same time. The divided soul that we discussed earlier, when we gave it the name "incontinent" or "continent," doesn't have the same kind of harmony.

When applied to friends, this doesn't necessarily mean that you should only be friends with people who are just like you, which would be pretty boring. It means that your wishes and goals for one another and the friendship you share are the same. On the other hand, having somewhat similar taste in some things wouldn't hurt—if one of you only had fun while fishing, and the other couldn't stand it, it might be challenging to spend a lot of time together.

In general, I would avoid making a broad statement about which comes "first," being friends with yourself or being friends with others. Yes, friendship with yourself in the sense of some portion of virtue is a kind of pre-requisite for friendship at all, but just the same, having good friends can be the most important motivating factor in trying to become a better person. So maybe the best approach is to try to walk with both of these feet and not worry about which one needs to take the first step.

Your Own Worst Enemy

"Wicked men seek for people with whom to spend their days, and shun themselves; for they remember many a grievous deed, and anticipate others like them, when they are by themselves, but when they are with others they forget. And having nothing lovable in them they have no feeling of love to themselves." (IX.4)

The opposite type of relationship to friendship is as ugly as the picture I painted above is pretty. If a good person does good for herself and her friend, and wants herself and her friend to exist, and shares life with herself and her friend, and has similar tastes and pleasures and pains as herself and her friend, the opposite is true of the wicked person. Someone consumed by greed or pride or jealousy or whatever is self-destructive, doing harm to her life and those around her. She doesn't share life with herself—if anything, she runs from life (as Aristotle describes in the quote above), and does whatever it takes to avoid thinking about it.

I talked a little while ago about Blaise Pascal and his idea of "diversion." Here Aristotle anticipates the same idea in its application to friendship. Instead of a mutual care and goodwill, a wicked friend uses the other for distraction. Rather than enhance life, the friend is a drug to make the pain go away, or a game to help one pretend the pain isn't there. When you're this kind of friend, the result isn't joyful and mutual upbuilding but rather a draining dependence that ends in resentment or in some other bad thing.

So a vicious person, because he harms himself, ends up harming his friend rather than doing good for him. He is pained at his own existence, being torn apart by his own passions, and therefore brings pain to his friends as well. He doesn't share life with himself but rather conflict, and this often extends to his friend, since he is too unsettled in his heart to be happy without drama.

If this hits your heart a little too deeply, many people have had this experience (both as the cause and the recipient of relationships like this) and I don't think this kind of thing is entirely uncommon. But it does hurt, on both sides. Like everything in ethics, what should be done in any given case is a complicated matter for prudence to decide, but Aristotle wouldn't have written his book, nor would I be writing mine, if there weren't a real hope for improvement. In a way, everything in both of these books is there to offer help for this problem.

How to Make Friends

"One may have goodwill both towards people whom one does not know, and without their knowing it." (IX.5)

I'm a pretty awkward being, for a lot of reasons, but one of them (I think) is the fact that my English was not-so-good (in that it was nonexistent) when I started school. This didn't only make conversation difficult, but I think I missed out on a lot of the basic social skills that kids learn in those first few years of school. Luckily, it's never too late to learn something new, and Aristotle is here to teach me how to make friends. I'm hoping we soon discover his lost treatise *On Not Picking Your Nose*.

Ok, so he doesn't actually have a chapter on how to make friends, but there is some implicit advice in Book IX that can teach us a lot. Most of the advice is actually embedded in his definition of friendship itself, which I will now heroically copy and paste from above to make your life easier as my beloved reader: *"recognized reciprocal goodwill."*

Like and help people (goodwill), have them like you (reciprocal), and let each other know that (recognized). So, step 1 in making friends is liking people and wanting what's good for them. This also fits into some definitions of the nebulous phrase "be nice." That might seem obvious, but it isn't to everyone. If you don't know that boy or girl who is mean to the boy or girl he or she likes, it's probably you. The semi-grown-up version of this naturally childish character flaw is the internet troll who acts surprised and offended when people hate him.

The weird thing about friendship is that because it's reciprocal, it needs the consent of the person you want to be friends with, which means in order to be liked you have to be likeable. You can't force someone to like you, because force is by definition an act of violence, and violence is an unnatural movement, and friendship is a natural one. Even if you like someone a ton and truly want what's best for them with all your heart, that doesn't make them your friend. If they don't reciprocate within a reasonable amount of time and interaction, that's the end of it. Move on and grow up. Nobody likes a pushy person, which means another important prerequisite for friendship is the ability to accept things you can't control.

So be nice, and if they're nice back, you're on the right track. What's left is recognition, which means you have to let each other know, which means you have to talk. So spending time talking is the way to make a friendship grow, which isn't surprising because you can't like or care about what you don't know. So be nice, do good things, take time and trouble to get to know each other, and when it's reciprocated you're on your way. Do this over time—don't rush. Good things are worth waiting for, and because friendship is based on the free will of both parties, be patient as they take their time too. That means don't act more friendly than you've earned. Friendship is worth the work and the wait, and even the work makes it more worth it: "men love what they have won by labor."

Figure 9: How to make friends

Against Altruism

> "If a man were always anxious that he himself, above all things, should act justly, temperately, or in accordance with any other of the virtues, and in general were always to try to secure for himself what is noble, no one would call such a man a lover of self or blame him." (IX.8)

In all fairness to altruism (which I critiqued earlier) there's something right about it if you understand it to be the opposite of "selfishness." If selfishness is a harmful thing, then unselfishness is a good thing. All that's fine until you start defining your terms. What we usually mean by selfish is doing whatever you want without caring about how it affects others. That's certainly a bad way to live, but Aristotle points out that it's also a harmful thing for the person being selfish. It's sort of the main theme of the entire *Nicomachean Ethics* that acting against reason hurts you first and foremost, and acting in a way that could hurt the people around you is against reason. You do have to live with them, after all, and if they're your friends, and a friend is another self, then hurting them is hurting yourself. So, if we follow his line of reasoning, that means selfish people don't even make themselves happy. And that's not very selfish of them.

But if you habitually act according to reason, are fair and kind to others, good to your friends, moderate in your actions, and you do all of this with the intent of making yourself happy, you're not selfish in any bad way. I really think that calling a person like that "selfish" in any negative sense is to miss the entire point of ethics. It's telling people that they should feel guilty for pursuing their own good, even if that good is good for everyone else as well. Describing that as a bad thing is an act of destruction. It would be much more productive to teach what I think is the truth: that each person's happiness is tied up with the happiness of the people around them, and that if you want to be happy, you can't do that without caring about the people around you being happy too.

The core of this idea shows up in Aristotle's understanding of a friend as another self, and especially in his idea that without friends, nobody could be happy. This seems to fulfill the promises he made in Book I about the common good and the purpose of the human being, and it also helps introduce the book Aristotle intends to be read after the *Ethics*, which is his *Politics*. It's not about beating people down with guilt or creating abstract principles of right and wrong to follow no matter what happens: it's about showing people that their pursuit of happiness requires them to share their life with others, or they won't have much happiness at all.

This also helps clarify the relationship between reason and the passions. Reason, when it's doing its job well, makes this conclusion about the connection between our individual good and the good of our community. The passions, when left unmoderated, are ultimately selfish in the bad sense, and satisfying them in an unmoderated way prevents us from caring about others. I could think of a hundred examples of this, from the greedy politician to the adulterous husband to the screaming toddler, but you probably have your own examples.

Life, Perception, Happiness

> "He must, therefore, perceive the existence of his friend together with his own, and this will be realized in their living together and sharing in discussion and thought, for this is what living together would seem to mean in the case of man, and not, as in the case of cattle, feeding in the same place." (IX.10)

What do we "get" out of living with friends that's so important that nobody would choose to live without friends, "even if he had every other good?" Let's try to tie it all together. From Book I we've been working with the idea that human life, in its particularity, is about thinking. We digest and reproduce, but plants do that as well. We see and smell and walk around, but animals do that too. So if we do this stuff and have what we need to do it as much as possible, we'd be living good plant or animal lives, but there would still be something missing if that's all we had and did.

If friendship is an essential part of human life, then it must have something to do with thinking and knowing and perception. This is where we add a second principle to the one I just mentioned. A friend is like another self—it's somebody you care about and know in a way similar to the way you care about and know yourself. Now for the third piece of the puzzle: it's not very easy to know or perceive yourself. This is easiest to illustrate with the senses—our eyes are built into our heads in a way that we can't look at our own faces without the aid of a mirror or camera or something. Knowing yourself in other ways seems to follow the same pattern. It's hard to know if you're being selfish or self-neglectful if you never interact with others. If you get lonely enough, you might even lose your sense of self entirely, or forget your own name like Gollum did.

Because of the difficulty of sensing or perceiving yourself when you're alone, you need a friend, because you can see a friend more easily than you can see yourself. Being with others, family and friends who care about you, is a source of real human life, that is, living like a human being rather than a vegetable or a cow. It's a wake up and a reminder of who you are, because the people you see are the same kind of being that you are, and if they're friends, that means by definition that they're like extensions of yourself. That's why true friendship is so rare and worth all the work and sacrifice and inconvenience and investment in the world. Without them you might drag yourself along for a while, from work to entertainment to sleep and back to work again, but that won't feel like enough because it's not enough.

Not only that, but with friends even the vegetable and animal stuff becomes human stuff. Eating a burger alone is nutrition. Eating with friends is a meal. I've had more meals alone than anybody I know, and I'm pretty well used to it and often prefer it. But there is something different about dinner with friends. Your perception of their perception makes everything brighter and more real, as if the salt became saltier with them around. The same goes for sense experiences. You can perceive a song or movie just fine on your own. But a song isn't a concert. You know very well by now that I'm as introverted as it gets, and I hate loud noise, but even I know there's something special about a concert, a kind of energy there in the crowd perceiving the band and each other, that isn't there in a recording. You'll get the same dialogue and plot watching a movie alone at home, but there's a different kind of goosebump you get when you hear a whole crowd laughing or cheering together, and a different kind of insight that you gain discussing the movie with your friends on the drive home from the theater. And if it's a good thing that you're sharing, it doesn't matter what it is—heavy metal music or comic books or philosophy or bench presses. If it's something you share with others in experience and conversation, it's something that creates real human friendship.

This isn't something I hear talked about a lot, but it seems extremely important. It's this kind of thing that really connects us to other people, that really allows us to "share" life itself, rather than the same living space or highways. It's in movies or concerts or fandoms or other communities that we perceive and think and know and feel together with others. So having friends and communities with common interests isn't a silly throwaway thing at the fringe of society that's only important because it can be profitable or it has some pacifying effect on cities or countries. This seems to be not only the heart of friendship but of human life itself.

Book X

Pleasure and Contemplation

In This Chapter:

Learning, feeling, doing, fun, awareness, politics.

Education

> "[Pleasure] is thought to be the most intimately connected with our human nature, which is the reason why in educating the young we steer them by the rudders of pleasure and pain." (X.1)

Since it's possible and pretty common for someone to have knowledge about living a good life but be unable to live one because of bad habits, Aristotle's understanding of education is more expansive than simply a transmission of knowledge. It's also more than a preparation to enter the workforce. For Aristotle, education was primarily about producing good people, and becoming a good person, as I hope I've illustrated already, requires more than just information and employability. Living a good life requires good habits of thinking, acting, and feeling, which means it requires practice and habituation. That habituation is one of the central roles of education in a city. And according to Aristotle, it is the job of the city as well as the family to educate people in virtue.

In other words, in order to become good citizens we need to learn how to care about one another. Some people (maybe?) are just caring by nature, and won't need much practice at all. Others (maybe?) just don't know that you're supposed to care about others, and once you tell them, your job as an educator is done. For everyone else (which I think is literally everyone), it takes practice to put our (bad) selfishness aside and truly care, with our mind, heart, and actions, about other people.

This is related to pleasure in two ways. As I've mentioned before, pleasure and pain are important tools to use in habituation. This isn't just about punishments, though learning to associate selfishness with bad things seems like it would be helpful in raising children. It's also about learning to have fun doing good things, things that are both self-fulfilling and good for the community around us. "Whistle while you work" is just as important as "you don't get to play Zegend of Lelda until you finish writing your paper."

Aristotle makes a very important point to both parents and politicians as they make rules for their families and cities: don't lie. If you tell your kids or your citizens that something is bad, and then you are caught doing it, or if it's such an obvious lie that nobody ever believes you, you've lost your moral authority over them, and harmed your very ability to be a parent or a community leader. It's a lot better to tell the truth—that some fun things can be harmful, and that you should be careful. Even better, you should lead others by example. I know lots of parents who are examples of this, and not a single politician.

What Pleasure Is Not

> "It seems to be clear, then, that neither is pleasure the good nor is all pleasure desirable, and that some pleasures are desirable in themselves." (X.3)

Some of this material on pleasure might seem repetitive, but it's coming within a different context than when we discussed it in earlier chapters. Before, we talked about how pleasure affects our actions, or how it's important in developing virtue, or how some pleasures need to be moderated. Here, something different is happening: Aristotle is working toward an actual definition of pleasure. As it turns out, pleasure is a difficult thing to define, and I'm not sure he really gives us a definition in the end. But that's okay—Aristotle doesn't give us definitions of some of his most important ideas, but his descriptions or his work toward definitions are still insightful, and might be enough for us to get the point. After all, ethics isn't as precise as some other sciences and doesn't need the same kind of clarity.

So we'll work toward an understanding of what pleasure is by first determining what it is not. The first thing it's not is "everything" or "everything important" or (as we discussed in Book I) "happiness itself." Aristotle shows this by doing a funny kind of math. If having pleasure is a good thing, but having pleasure *and* being wise is better, then wisdom adds to pleasure, which means pleasure isn't complete and total happiness by itself (since happiness, in Aristotle's view, is something complete). This tells us more about what Aristotle thinks of happiness than what he thinks of pleasure, but it's also a setup for something coming up soon: there is a sense in which happiness *is* pleasure, but only in a specific way. Let's keep taking a step at a time.

So pleasure isn't the highest or complete good, but on the other hand, pleasure is also not a bad thing. There are certainly some pleasures that are bad, or associated with harmful activities, but these examples of pleasure are not pleasure itself, and just because something can be bad sometimes doesn't mean that it's always bad or is a bad thing. In fact, Aristotle would say that bad pleasures, the ones that accompany harmful activities, aren't really pleasures at all. We're not yet equipped to see his argument for this, but it's good to note that, despite his anti-pleasure leaning in earlier Books, Aristotle ends up endorsing pleasure in the highest way.

This is a little more difficult to understand, but Aristotle makes it a point to argue that pleasure is also not a "change" or "movement." His argument for this is even more difficult to grasp than his point, but the application of this principle becomes important later, when he argues that happiness and pleasure are in a sense the same. The basic idea is, again, that the best kind of pleasure is somehow complete, and changes or movements are incomplete things. Pleasure is a way of "being," rather than a kind of "becoming." Like I said, this is weird but hold on to it for a few pages and we'll see what he does with it.

Pleasure is not, also, simply a bodily thing. This is because, while the body is certainly involved in many (if not all) pleasures, it's not the body that feels them but rather the whole person. Some pleasures are more bodily than others, but the thing that feels is you, not your body or some body part alone. Pleasure is something that is related to a whole person—so even if your feet feel good during a foot rub, *you* feel your feet feeling good. Pleasure, and especially the kind of pleasure that *is* happiness, is something that you do in the totality of your being.

What Pleasure Is

"Without activity pleasure does not arise, and every activity is completed by the attendant pleasure." (X.4)

Let's say you've decided to pick up mandolin playing. You go to the store and buy a mandolin that's moderately priced—too cheap and it'll sound awful and be hard to play; too expensive is imprudent since you're not sure you'll stick with it and make it worth the investment. But you shell out some money, and it's painful. Then you tune it and start plucking. But you don't have calluses yet on your fingers, and mandolin strings are razor sharp, so it's painful. Then you check out some YouTube videos on "mandolin exercises for beginners," and you have to sit there and play boring scales back and forth with developing calluses, which is painful. Then you get decent enough to play an actual song, and you find one you like, but you can't play it fast enough for it to sound good. You sit there and mess up the same note every time, and pause in the middle of it, and after a while you get sick of it and don't even enjoy the melody as much as you used to. And all this is painful. Do this for a few months, or years, and develop a habit, refine your talent, and practice every day. Someday, there will be pleasure involved.

Again, I'm not sure Aristotle ever really gives us a definition of pleasure. The closest he gets is "something that accompanies activity." This is a little confusing, but I do think he's on to something. Activity (which is another thing Aristotle never really defines) is when we do what we're able to do. This sounds like a pointless thing to say, but ability is an important part of this picture. We all have a ton of abilities within ourselves—some might argue that all we are is a combination of different abilities or capacities or "powers." Those abilities can go unused, or we can activate them by activity. When we activate them, the fulfillment of whatever ability we're activating is accompanied by pleasure. A massage is pleasurable because the skin activates its ability to feel as it's being touched. A song is pleasurable because the ears activate their ability to hear and the mind activates its ability to savor a melody. A movie is pleasurable (even when it's sad) because the soul activates its ability to recognize something true about reality in the story and characters, and knowing the truth is (if Aristotle is right) the best ability we have.

Of course, if the activity is way out of proportion or badly done, there is less pleasure or even pain. If the massage is too forceful it hurts; if the music is too loud or the melody doesn't synchronize at all with your feelings, it's painful rather than pleasant. If the movie is incomprehensible or lousy, it's not very fun to watch at all. If your hands are too big to play the mandolin, or if your fingers haven't gotten tough enough to hold down the strings yet, or if you haven't developed the habit capable of playing a whole song without messing up, there is less and less pleasure, because the activity isn't quite proportional to the abilities you have. Practice really just means working on your abilities so that you can later do what you can't do now. It's pain in the present for the sake of pleasure in the future.

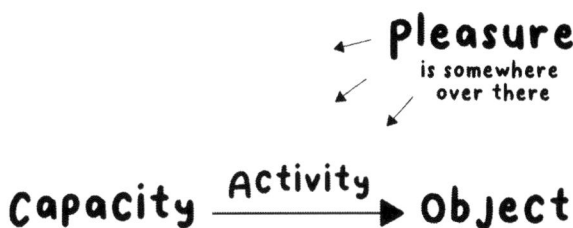

pleasure
is somewhere
over there

Capacity —Activity→ **Object**

Figure 10: Where pleasure is

Two Kinds of Pleasure

"The activities of thought differ from those of the senses, and both differ among themselves, in kind; so, therefore, do the pleasures that complete them." X.5

We have a kind of working description of pleasure as "the thing that also happens when you do stuff good." But the fact is we can do a lot of stuff, and even within each of the things we can do, there is a lot of stuff that can be the object of the doing. We can see and hear and taste and walk and lift weights and think, but we can also see green and swimming pools and turbans. And not all doings are pleasurable, nor is everything we look at pleasant. How do we make sense of all this? Why are some activities fun and some not?

Well, as we saw in the last section, some activities aren't quite suited to us or we to them—I don't quite enjoy playing mandolin as much as I might if I keep practicing for a few months. Other pleasures are mixed with pain, for example we might be enjoying a walk outside talking to a friend, but it might be really hot outside. We're actualizing our ability to walk and have a conversation, and those activities are pleasant because they're proportioned to our ability, but the temperature isn't proportioned to our ability to feel temperature since it's hotter than we'd like. In general, we can say that the body's organs are an important reference point to the proportionality of activities we're capable of. Our eyes determine both the brightness and the wavelengths of light that we're able to see, and similarly with our other organs. Things outside of the ranges determined by these organs, or even on the edge, wouldn't normally be very pleasant to us. In general, the pain of one capacity can stunt the pleasure of another. If our beloved grandmother is sick, it will be hard for us to enjoy a sunset the same way.

We also get bored of doing the same thing, even when that thing was fun to begin with. That might also be connected to the organs and their role in feeling pleasure. Our skin perceives touch when it's pressed by something—the change in its state is what caused the sense of touch to activate. But if the state stays the same, the feeling fades, like when we stop noticing a consistent background noise. Some things we just get used to in general, and therefore get bored of, and the pleasure we took in them gradually goes away. I remember moving to Oakland and seeing the mountains in California, and thinking I'd never get tired of looking at them. That lasted a few months, and now mountains are just another thing. This might help explain why we like new activities and games and why we enjoy travel.

There does seem to be a difference between some capacities and others in this, and Aristotle makes a point that the more intellectual powers suffer less from this kind of weariness. Looking at the color green might have been amazing at some point in your life, and then it became just another color, and colors became just another thing. But thinking about justice, even if it's difficult, doesn't seem to get boring in the same way for those capable of enjoying it. I teach Plato's *Republic* every single year, and I haven't gotten bored of it yet. And maybe your spouse's face isn't as eye-catching as when you first met at that pub, but hopefully their personality is just as interesting.

In general, then, Aristotle groups all our different perceptive capacities into two broad categories: those of the senses and those of the intellect. Hearing, seeing, and smelling are all different, but they are all senses with organs that directly interact with particular sensible things in the world. Thinking and knowing are certainly tied to sensible perception (since, for Aristotle, everything we know is through the senses), but their objects aren't directly sensible. So we can only look at a bright light for so long before our eyes get tired or hurt, but we can think of brightness as much as we want.

If you accept this broad categorization, you might follow Aristotle's next point, which is that in general the intellectual and sensible capacities can often be in competition with each other. If you're at a loud concert it's probably hard for you to read and understand a book. Aristotle's example is of a flute player performing in the middle of a philosophy class and distracting the students, which is kind of a funny scenario if it actually happened. I don't have any actual study to back this up, but I'd guess that people eat more popcorn in proportion to how bad a movie is, and less if the movie is so absorbing that they can't look away.

Feeling Good

> "The pleasure proper to a worthy activity is good and that proper to an unworthy activity is bad." (X.5)

We've framed the internal conflict most people feel as one between "reason" and "the passions," though there are many ways to phrase it. Some religions (including my own) use the word "temptation" for the conflict and "sin" for when the passions win. Dostoevsky has Dimitri Karamazov describe himself as both an "angel" and a "cockroach." Here at the end of the *Nicomachean Ethics* Aristotle gives us a pretty sophisticated new set of concepts to understand what's going on. Because we are made up of many different abilities/capacities/powers, and each of them is the basis for a corresponding activity, and each activity comes with a corresponding pleasure, it's possible for one power to conflict with another.

Some pleasures are pretty tame and therefore don't get in the way of much. You might be super into cologne, for example, but it's unlikely that you'll lose your job because you skip work for weeks at a time to go to the store and smell cologne. But other activities bring more intense pleasures, and that intensity means they can cause conflict with other activities, or even overcome them, including the activity of the reasoning power. The pleasure we get from thinking is beautiful and real, but it's subtle and easy to miss if there are more intense ones around. Aristotle says that nobody could really do philosophy while they're having sex, though some philosophies might lend themselves to that more than others. Even within the same sense activity, subtle things are often missed. If I paid fifty bucks for a fancy steak, you can bet that I won't be putting any hot sauce on it. And I put hot sauce on everything. Especially pizza.

These intense activities that correspond to intense pleasures can understandably gain a strong hold on us. This is how addictions can begin, and lives can be destroyed; more moderately, this is how days are wasted on video games while books and mandolins and friendships get neglected. Then things get really messy, because the intense pleasure gets boring and wearisome like everything else, and a more intense one is required. The senses and the ability of perception itself can get blown out and become dysfunctional. Jesus tells the story of a rich man and a poor man named Lazarus who died on his porch. The punchline there is that the rich man didn't notice Lazarus because he was too busy partying every day. The pleasure of helping others is one of the most sublime things we can experience in life, but it's a subtle and delicate thing, and can't be heard over loudspeakers.

If any of this is true, our conclusion should at least be to be careful and sparing with super-intense pleasures if we want to retain balance over the rest of our lives. You might even make yourself a rule when you're thinking clearly, and try your best to follow it. Some examples include "no ice cream till you've worked out," "no video games till you've done your homework," and "no sex until marriage." You're not doing anybody but yourself a favor when you live this way—according to reason. Remember, it's the job of the virtue of prudence to decide which capacity is activated at any given time, and prudence needs a clear mind to do its job right.

Two extreme examples can help illustrate my point. A professional musician or athlete is someone who has refined their capacities with strong habits to the point of near perfection, and when they do what they're trained to do, their soul reaches an amazing kind of unity. Their body, emotions, actions, will, and mind are all focused and unified. When a great musician plays, or a great athlete athletes, I bet the kind of pleasure that accompanies their activity is indescribable, because it's the pleasure accompanying the activity of basically every power of their soul working together. It's something so amazing that it's pleasant even to watch from the outside. Contrast this with the conflicted addict that we all know and maybe we've all been at one point or another. Their mind is tortured knowing that they are living a life of self-destruction, but their addiction causes them pain when they don't indulge it. At every moment there is blinding hurt in them in one place or another, and the pleasure of one capacity is the pain of another. Yes, the athlete and musician had to put in a lot of painful hours to get where they are, but I think it's worth it. It might really be the only way to live a happy life—not being an athlete or musician, but working to unify yourself so that all of your mind and soul can act and feel as one.

It's not just unity though. Remember that the vicious person is just as unified as the virtuous one. The activity that is happiness is one where the whole person is unified under the leadership of reason. This goes all the way back to the argument at the beginning of the book, which discussed why reasoning is the characteristic human activity. Here we return to it again at the end. It is the act of thinking that makes our actions truly human actions, and truly pleasant. We are of course capable, through bad habits, of enjoying things that are inhumanly bad. But an act isn't good or reasonable just because it's enjoyed. That enjoyment can simply mean that the person feeling the enjoyment is in a sick kind of state, like someone with a cold thinking something as boring as chicken soup tastes good.

Work and Amusement

> "It would, indeed, be strange if the end were amusement, and one
> were to take trouble and suffer hardship all one's life in order to amuse
> oneself." (X.6)

Bringing all our capacities together in a focused activity might be a helpful hint at the kind of things we can do that are close to happiness. Remember that happiness isn't a state or a possession but an activity, and we can better understand this now with Aristotle's description of pleasure. So if happiness is an activity that somehow brings together many or all of our capacities, we might be on the right track.

On the other hand, there are all kinds of things that we can do that are like that. When I'm translating (especially something interesting), I often become so focused that I lose track of time; my mind, my eyes, my typing hands, my memory, all work together, and sometimes I don't notice things going on around me or the fact that I'm speaking out loud. It's an activity that I've spent a lot of time on, and a habit that I have pretty deeply ingrained in me. And, to top it off, it's really fun. But even if it's part of the happiness I have in my life at times, I'm not sure I'd say that for me translating *is* happiness, even subjectively just for me. There are other things that I do that have the same effect on me. Sometimes playing music does that; sometimes reading; sometimes even writing this awful book. Whatever happiness is might be the thing that all these activities have in common with each other.

There is one thing that can partially ruin things, though. When there is a real, dire necessity depending on these activities, I might be able to do them nearly as well, but the pressing need is a kind of weight that can act as a distraction. It's still fun to translate even when I get paid for it (which is extremely rare), but it's not quite the same. I've never needed to play mandolin or write an essay to save someone's life, but I can imagine it wouldn't be as fun. Physical necessity might be a good motivator for you to get things done, but that does make the activity "work," and if your rent depends on it there's a bit of a drag on the pleasure that accompanies it—especially if there's a boss constantly breathing down your neck. That, of course, is assuming you have a job where you do something you really love in the first place, which is already pretty rare. I think all this is the case because happiness is the purpose of life, and making money and survival aren't final ends, but means to an end. We make money so that we can become happy, which is something other than making money.

On the other side there's amusement or recreation, which Aristotle sees as absolutely necessary for life because work is a strain that needs to be relaxed periodically. Even if we love what we do, we can't do it all the time, probably for the reasons I talked about a few pages ago. So we need to do something different to refresh ourselves. And if we spend a lot of our time just making ends meet financially, that's one of the activities that we need a break from. We need to do things that don't make money if we're going to keep our sanity. That's what vacations, games, and nights out are for.

And amusements can also be activities that really bring together a lot of our capacities in a focused way. So they have something in common with happiness, assuming we're on the right track with all this. On the other hand, the activity of happiness was first defined (way back at the beginning) as the purpose of life itself, and it would be weird if the meaning of life were playing Jenga and going on roller coasters, much less doing both at the same time. Games don't hurt anyone, but they're by definition not serious. They're also somewhat self-centered, possibly in the negative sense. Amusements are necessary and important, but making them the center of our lives seems ultimately childish and selfish. Happiness, the activity that is the purpose of the human being, can't be either of those things: it has to be the activity of a mature person rather than a childish one, and the activity of a social being, since that's an important part of who we are.

So we're looking for an activity that is serious but not necessary for survival. We recreate (among other reasons) so that we can work, and we work so that we can have a house and food, but why do we do any of those things? The word Aristotle uses to answer that question is "leisure." Leisure isn't the same as amusement and it's not the same as work. It's serious activity that we do without needing to do it. It's an alien concept to a lot of us today, and there's a pretty good book about it by Josef Pieper that you should read when you have a chance. But I'll do my best to describe it here.

Contemplation

"But we must not follow those who advise us, being men, to think of human things, and, being mortal, of mortal things, but must, so far as we can, make ourselves immortal, and strain every nerve to live in accordance with the best thing in us." (X.7)

Leisure is not just an academic or intellectual thing. It's the thing that's common to amusement and to work, the element that makes both of them pleasurable. It's the activity of thoughtfulness itself, when we do it just to do it. To be precise, leisure is the name for the possibility of this kind of thoughtful activity, and the activity itself is called contemplation. What exactly Aristotle means by this isn't totally clear, but that might be more of an exegetical question, and ethics is a practical science. What does it mean, practically speaking, that the activity that is happiness is contemplation?

"Sitting there thinking super hard but like not for money, for fun" might not be your idea of happiness. On the other hand, thoughtfulness isn't just the characteristic human activity in some abstract philosophical sense. It really is there whenever we do something well: when we make a decision, or have a nice meal with a friend, or listen to a song, or watch a movie, or look at the ocean. Contemplation isn't writing an essay, though it's involved whenever we do that; it isn't being a professional academic or a cloistered nun, though probably those lifestyles involve a lot of it. It's there when we garden or take a deep breath after a stressful meeting, and when we look at a painting or lose our train of thought while driving on an empty highway at night.

It's the thing that we lose when a moment of lust overtakes us, or greed causes us to become jealous and obsess over someone else's success; it's destroyed when we're anxious and afraid, and it's what we get back when those things go away. In order to have it every day, we need some share in all the virtues, a stable character, and all the necessities of life—though being too rich would probably hurt, since wealth comes with too many responsibilities and distractions. It's the thing we can do best when we're spending quality time with good friends, and what's there when all the noise goes away and we're left with ourselves, provided we don't hate ourselves and have healed from our tortured past.

If the basic idea is that the highest capacity we have is thoughtfulness, that capacity is the definitive one that sets us apart as a species. That capacity and activity provides the highest possible pleasure, the pleasure that is happiness by definition, and even though we can't do it all the time, it's the thing that gives purpose to everything else we do. We make money and vote and live in cities and make friends and develop good habits, all so that we can live thoughtful, contemplative lives. We do everything we do so that we can exist in this way—by being able to know that we exist, and savor that thought.

But, to be fair to both Aristotle and much of the tradition that followed him, human existence isn't the best possible object of thought. It's a good thing to know you exist, just as it's a good thing to know the universe or some aspect of it. These are fitting objects of contemplation, and good things to think about. But part of an activity is its object. We eat, but our best eating is done with the best food—the food that is best suited to us, our digestive organs, our taste buds, our health. Our best thinking is also done with the best object, and for Aristotle, this object is God (maybe with a lowercase g, but that's a debate I won't go into). Again, what Aristotle exactly meant by God is a complicated (and pretty weird) thing, but our topic is practical living, not textual exegesis. Aristotle's final definition of happiness is the activity of contemplating God, or doing something as close to that as we can, as often as we can, and everything else in life is there for us to do that, whatever that might mean. This kind of contemplation is also, notably, the kind of activity that Aristotle thinks God does all the time.

I am a priest you know. You didn't think I'd mention this at some point?

Politics

"What argument would remold such people?" (X.9)

All this being said, contemplation is only half the picture, even if it is the better half. Remember that the human being had two related definitions: rational animal and social animal. The thing that defines us, the mind, isn't just a floating ghostly intellect, but is also the thing that connects us to other people. The moral virtues that guide our daily life are just as human as the intellectual virtues that govern contemplation, and they are accordingly the source of true pleasure. Living well with others, in justice and moderation, caring about them and our larger communities, is a source of real happiness that can't be neglected—and that's why Aristotle doesn't, but ends the *Nicomachean Ethics* by introducing his next book, the *Politics*.

He even introduces a question that he doesn't resolve until the *Politics* about which way of life is best of all, that of contemplation or that of political activity, especially political leadership. Even though the contemplative life ends up winning that contest, the political life wins in its own way by being more practically necessary. In other words, the philosopher (or by extension the thoughtful person in general) lives a happier life, but the good politician lives a more useful life for others. Philosophy is godly in its object and activity, but politics is godly in its influence and the amount of good it can accomplish for the community.

It's almost laughable to imagine a virtuous politician, much less a thoughtful one (Plato presents a law about a "philosopher king" as needed but ultimately absurd in the *Republic*). The fact that it's so rare isn't a surprise. Politicians need to be famous or at least well known, and often (depending on the elective process) need a lot of money. That alone requires a complicated and often-disturbed lifestyle that doesn't lend itself to virtuous living, much less contemplation. A philosopher, or just a thoughtful person living a thoughtful but relatively private life, doesn't need fame or a lot of money to do what they do, and there is therefore greater possibility for peace and leisure.

But even though the political life is relatively unhappy, somebody has to do it. Having nobody lead is just an invitation to anarchy and warlords fighting over sections of land with wandering tribes of shirtless barbarians. The good and happy life described in this entire book requires a well-governed city or country. Without it, basic survival is barely possible, much less good living. So the book ends where it began—with the common good, and the reminder that your happiness is dependent on, and somehow less important than, the good of all. The *Epic of Gilgamesh* begins and ends with a description of the walls of the city Uruk, walls built by the king who began his story selfish and uncivilized but ended it connected to his people and accepting his responsibilities as a leader.

The story of politics is a different one from that of ethics, but the two are connected. Leading others toward virtue and a good life requires first that you know what they are—and that you live them yourself. But the particular complexity of political life is that leadership is not the same as philosophical training. Learning what happiness is and living it is different from teaching it to others, and you can tell people to care about each other and be thoughtful till you're out of breath, but having them listen to you is a totally different thing. Argumentation, even if it's perfect, isn't a thing that convinces a lot of people, as you know if you've ever been on the internet. Individuals might be teachable by conversation, but communities learn by habituation, and habituation is established by good laws. But that's a long story, and not my problem. For now, you might not be able to change the world right away, but you can begin by working on yourself, and then move on to helping your family, friends, and community.

What Next?

This book, like the book it's based on, isn't about knowledge but action. So if you learned anything from it, read the book it's based on. Then go do something.

In Defense of Popular Writing

Originally a post on younan.blog from 4/23/2020

The Danger of Caring about Non-Scholars

I know I'm not the only one who was told by academic friends to "hold off" on writing popular-level books until I was "established" by some indiscriminate number of works published by high-level academic journals or publishers. This advice was given to me as stating a material fact of life in academia today: popular books are generally looked down upon by Real Academics, and one should avoid writing them until one has earned the credentials of a Real Academic. Outside the graduate school bubble, one would naively think that the earning of a doctorate is exactly such a credential. But competition for academic jobs and book deals is fierce, and people with graduate degrees are more abundant than ever, so decision-makers in universities and publishing houses look for other ways to set apart the scholars that will get the jobs and the deals.

Fair enough. You want scholars that are serious about their fields of expertise, who engage it with originality and creativity and say something new, something that sets them apart from other scholars. You want research and contribution. Like it or not, though, that means you get specialization. That's just math. This many scholars writing means longer and longer essay titles describing smaller and smaller ideas. "The big ideas have all been ideated," so the saying goes that I just made up, and so we must pursue the smaller ones, the cracks left behind by the generations before, who were privileged enough to live during a time when there was still something left to say.

The problem is that the average Josephus doesn't care about the cracks. The scholars barely care, and sometimes I wonder if they're just pretending. But if you write for Joe, you don't make a contribution to the field of minute crack analysis, and the university administrator who has no idea what any applicant's dissertation is about decrees that you do not get the job.

The Injustice of Not Caring

What we're left with is way too many academic journals, which means an ocean of secondary literature to swim through before you can write the first sentence of the essay you need to have written to add another drop to the ocean to put it on your CV to make it two lines longer so it looks a little more impressive to the recruiter as she's skimming through applications.

Hyperbole (?) aside, a more principled problem is that even though academic research of all kinds is a noble end in itself, that end is not something isolated from the good of the community at large. Scholarship is an end in itself, but scholars are not. We are citizens just like everyone else, and it seems to me that we owe it to our communities to relay the fruits of scholarship to them in whatever form we can. It is only because of the city that the university exists in the first place, and it seems a serious injustice for universities to draw nourishment from the soil of cities without bearing some fruit for them. Translated in the cheapest possible way, that means the taxpayers investing in schools deserve something for their money.

This happens more easily with STEM subjects, since technological advancement is a kind of good that the culture at large can enjoy pretty easily. But humanities departments are meant to bear fruit as well, and I'm not talking about some generic community outreach. I wouldn't buy a car from Ghiradelli or chocolate from Chevy. The fruit of humanities departments, the thing they're supposed to be good at, is ideas. When those ideas are so refined that they are invisible to the nonspecialist, we have a case of a tree whose fruit can only be eaten by the tree itself. This is an unnatural arrangement. It's also a pretty recent one, since world-class scholars of their own time had no compunction writing for popular audiences. Mortimer Adler comes to mind, as well as Aquinas's *Compendium of Theology*, Augustine's *Sermons*, and Aristotle's *Rhetoric*. There are still scholars doing this today, but they are generally both rare and already well-established.

My Proposal

I'm not proposing that we abolish or discourage scholarly publishing. I'm proposing that we (meaning academics and academic institutions) encourage popular writing among scholars. Writing on big ideas in a way that many people can read should not be a shameful thing. But we all know that it is. We can and should change that. And if this COVID quarantine is really as dangerous for colleges as people are saying, public displays of relevance are all the more critical.

Here's why you, the scholar, should write more popular works:

Reason 1: It's good for you

It's refreshing to the mind to attempt to explain a fancy idea to a non-specialist. It puts things in a different light. Using plain old English instead of academic jargon requires a kind of clarity that can be lost in academic writing. There is admittedly a difference between academic and popular writing, but the difference can be seen as complementary rather than in tension. Popular writing can be a change of scenery, rather than a drudgery, after which you return to academic work renewed.

Reason 2: If scholars don't do it, amateurs will

That will mean that the "intellectual middle class" is left with mediocrity, or worse. This is bad for everyone, since research departments in universities are, despite their best efforts, located on the surface of planet earth, in the midst of a civilization populated by non-specialists. And when everyone around you gets the wrong idea because you didn't want to explain the right idea to them, it's *your* fault. In fact:

Reason 3: You don't get to complain about where "society is headed" when you're doing nothing about it

Scholarship is meant to be a guiding light, but if your only contribution is thirty pages of dense analysis in the next volume of *The New Yearbook for Phenomenology and Phenomenological Philosophy*, your light won't reach many people.

Reason 4: It will encourage people to major in your field

Nobody starts off in a field by reading top-tier scholarly articles. They start with pop books. If these books are good, they read more. The more people like this there are, the more likely you'll get some majors out of them, and the more likely your department will stay open.

Reason 5: Honestly, it's probably much more interesting than what you're writing now

Maybe you're not stuck in a rut, or paralyzed with writer's block. Maybe the stuff you're thinking about is just really boring. If it is, which is more likely the more specialized it is, that might also mean your classes are boring, which might be why students avoid them. It might also be why humanities departments are viewed as disconnected from reality and living in an ivory tower. Humanities are the most important things in the world. We who teach them know it. It's our job to reveal that to everyone else.

In the interest of fairness, I present two possible obstacles to my proposal, along with my impolite and dismissive responses:

Problem 1: Scholars aren't good at writing in a way comprehensible to nonspecialists

That might mean that they don't really understand what they think they understand. Or it might mean that there's nothing there to understand in the first place.

Problem 2: Some ideas can't be written in a way comprehensible to nonspecialists

Try harder. Werner Heisenberg, Albert Einstein, Niels Bohr, and many others wrote popular-level books on quantum mechanics and general relativity. These books are still in print today, and they're great reading. They are both deeper and more readable than whatever you're working on. Figure it out.

Even though it's often abused by admins and people who don't like reading, I wonder if the "ivory tower" stigma doesn't have some truth to it, and whether scratching each other's backs as we quote and footnote ourselves into the stratosphere might be more suffocating than liberating. Maybe it would be healthy for an increasingly sickly academia to let its feet touch the ground again. Anyway, what else are we supposed to do during the six months we're waiting to hear back from an academic publisher?

For Further Study

Go to a used bookstore, find a copy of Aristotle's *Nicomachean Ethics*, and read it.

Also these look pretty good:

What Would Aristotle Do? Self-Control through the Power of Reason by Elliot D. Cohen (Prometheus, 2003).

The Consolations of Philosophy by Alain de Botton (Vintage International, 2000).

Aristotle's Way: How Ancient Wisdom Can Change Your Life by Edith Hall (Penguin, 2019).

Living the Good Life: A Beginner's Thomistic Ethics by Steven J. Jensen (Catholic University of America Press, 2013).

The Socrates Express: In Search of Life Lessons from Dead Philosophers by Eric Weiner (Avid Reader Press, 2020).

Printed in Great Britain
by Amazon